Acknowledgements

Hundreds of teachers and thousands of children have participated in the National Writing Project. They have been supported by many local advisers, members of higher education colleges, parents and others in the community. We cannot name them all, but we would like to acknowledge the commitment of those participants, and trust that these publications represent at least some of their views about classroom practice.

The National Writing Project was set up by the School Curriculum Development Committee. Its three-year Development Phase (1985-1988) directly involved twenty-four local authorities and was funded jointly by the School Curriculum Development Committee and the LEAs. In 1988, the National Curriculum Council took responsibility for the Project's final implementation year.

Central Project Team (Development Phase 1985-1988)

Pam Czerniewska: Director

Eve Bearne
Barbara Grayson   } Project Officers
John Richmond
Jeremy Tafler

Naomi Baker
Anne Hogan   } Administrators
Judy Phillips

Central Project Team (Implementation Phase 1988-1989)

Jeremy Tafler: Director

Georgina Herring   } Project Officers
Marie Stacey

Rosemary Robertson: Administrator

Steering Committee

Andrew Wilkinson: Chair

Dennis Allen
Peter Andrews
Iain Ball
Douglas Barnes
Pat Barrett
Eunice Beaumont
Peter Boulter
Harold Gardiner
Alan Hall
David Halligan
John Johnson
Gulzar Kanji
Keith Kirby
Maggie Maclure
Colin Smith
June Thexton
Jenny Taylor
Mike Torbe
Janet White

Felicity Taylor: NCC Reader

Local Project Co-ordinators

Avon	Richard Bates
Bedfordshire	Mary Heath
Berkshire	Audrey Gregory
	Barry Pope
Birmingham	Ann Davis
	Sylvia Winchester
Cheshire	Gill Fox
	John Huddart
Cleveland	Margaret Meek
	Joan Sedgewicke
Croydon	Sheila Freeman
	Iain Weir
Dorset	Barbara Tilbrook
	Margaret Wallen
Dudley	Chris Morris
Durham	Dot Yoxall
Gwynedd	Len Jones
	Esyllt Maelor
	Nia Pierce Davies
Hampshire	Robin Culver
	Cath Farrow
	Ann Heslop
	Roger Mulley
Humberside	Sylvia Emerson
ILEA	Helen Savva
Manchester	Helen Henn
	Georgina Herring
Mid Glamorgan	Richard Landy
Newcastle	Jay Mawdsley
Rochdale	Frances Clarke
	Peter Phethean
	Vivienne Rowcroft
SCEA	Stuart Dyke
Sheffield	Sue Horner
Shropshire	Ned Ratcliffe
Somerset	Vernon Casey
	Maisie Foster
	Carole Mason
Staffordshire	Sallyanne Greenwood
Wiltshire	Gill Clarkson
	Sue Dean
	Jo Stone

We are particularly grateful to Joan Swann from the Open University School of Education for her help in preparing this material.

Contents

Introduction

Hundreds of teachers throughout England and Wales have taken part in the National Writing Project, and their ideas for developing children's writing have been published locally and nationally. If, as a result, more children are encouraged to write creatively and enthusiastically, many of the Project's aims will have been fulfilled. But is it enough to encourage children to write — albeit enthusiastically? In an effort to motivate children, should we give them increased freedom to write whatever they want to, or does this lead to a narrow selection of stereotyped topics?

This Theme Pack contains examples of work from the National Writing Project which demonstrate teachers' concerns about girls' and boys' writing. There are two main areas of concern: that the range of activities and topics selected by girls and boys respectively is unnecessarily restricted; and that the material which children read promotes gender stereotyping, which is reproduced in their own writing. Such aspects of children's writing cannot be considered in isolation. There is now a well established literature on gender and education, and the attention which teachers and researchers have begun to pay to gender in relation to writing forms part of a wider preoccupation with gender differences and inequalities. Some of this work is referred to in the text, and there is a set of notes and sources on page 63 for those interested in following up any of the issues.

Producing a document on the effects of gender bias on writing and learning has proved difficult. Teachers involved in the National Writing Project did not gather together specifically to discuss gender issues until the second year; we then found that we needed to spend time examining our own and society's prejudices and assumptions before we felt we could begin to try things out in the classroom. For some time we were uncertain about what we might actually do; it was difficult to formulate questions which might help teachers and pupils to identify and examine gender bias. As our awareness increased we began to record the work we did, and these case studies are included here. There are not as many as we might wish, partly because of our uncertainties and partly because this issue was not brought to the fore at the outset of the Project. For these reasons we have also included articles presenting a more broadly based overview, raising issues which encourage us to reflect upon and evaluate our practice.

As teachers we need opportunities to reflect and discuss; we need sources of information to which we can turn when we become frustrated. Examining an issue in a way which makes us question our own way of life is often painful; we hope that by admitting to the painfulness of the process other teachers will be able to cross the threshold.

'Traditionally the approach to teaching reading and writing has required passive co-operation. There has been much filling in of worksheets, sitting still to listen to stories, reading quietly, phonic drills and language exercises, sitting quietly (and alone) to write a story, learning spellings. So, if girls do better than boys at these activities, it should not surprise us, but this approach leaves both sexes as the losers.'[1]

'When I started teaching I felt there was a lot to be gained from reading, discussing and writing poetry . . . There was resistance. It quickly became clear that boys didn't readily identify with poetry . . .

'Mike Rosen came to school and read to children and parents, effectively

dispelling uncertainty some parents had about the place of poetry in the curriculum and showing the boys that "real men do write poetry"!' [2]

Girls' and boys' choices

This conversation took place between an adult and a four-year-old girl:

Adult: *'You could be the doctor.'*

Girl: *'No, I'm the nurse. A girl can't be a doctor.'*

Adult: *'Yes, she can. Barbara's a doctor.'*

Girl: *'No, I can't be a doctor. I'm a nurse.'*

. . . and this was from a three-year-old girl:

'I can kick and kick with these shoes 'cos these are boys' shoes.'

From birth, most children are categorised as either female or male: girls and boys are given different names; they have different clothes and hairstyles; on birthdays and at Christmas they receive different cards and presents. People react differently to boys and girls, even as babies. One of the more interesting pieces of research involved dressing the same babies alternately in girls' and boys' clothing. They were treated differently according to perceived gender; they were given different toys to play with, for instance, and the 'boys' were more often encouraged in 'gross motor activity'.[3]

At school the learning of behaviour which is considered socially appropriate continues: girls and boys engage in different activities; they behave and speak differently in the playground and in the classroom; teachers respond differently to girls and boys (sometimes behaviour that is accepted from boys is condemned in girls); and several classroom routines, such as calling the register and lining up separately, subtly reinforce gender distinctions.

It is important in any discussion of differences between girls' and boys' behaviour, or teachers' responses, to bear in mind that gender differences are always average ones. Boys may tend to behave in one way and girls in another, but there are exceptions to the general rule: there is an overlap between the sexes.

Gender distinctions are often felt to be disadvantageous to girls, but this is not to say that girls do less well academically, at least not in any straightforward way. In terms of their performance in standardised attainment tests, or passes in public examinations at 16+, girls do at least as well as boys and often slightly better. The gap that used to exist between the performances of girls and boys at 'A' Level is steadily being eroded. However, girls tend to avoid certain subjects, such as Mathematics and the physical sciences, and they do less well than boys after leaving school in terms of their choice of career and their participation in higher education. While no one can hold schools uniquely responsible for gender inequalities in society, many people have argued that schools reinforce such inequalities when they could be trying to alleviate them.[4]

Evidence that girls and boys tend to approach writing differently has to be considered in the light of such research. Girls prefer, and tend to do better than boys at language-related activities, including writing. Many people have argued that schools need to ensure a balanced selection of activities, encouraging boys to participate more in language work (amongst other things) and girls in Mathematics, Technology and other male-dominated subjects. The Equal Opportunities Commission suggests that such encouragement needs to begin early:

'It is very important, in both academic and human terms, that young children should have the opportunity to develop the full range of learning skills. In an era of increasing scientific and technological development, a confident approach towards Mathematics, Science and Information Technology will become increasingly important for all children, whilst at the same time, the ability to communicate and to care for one another will become more and more essential.' [5]

The NATE Language and Gender Committee's description of GCSE English coursework folders[6] illustrates girls' and boys' preferences in subject matter for their writing:

	Jill's assignments	*Jack's assignments*
Narrative:	Boy meets girl	Raid on the bank
Discursive:	Letters to an agony column on relationships with parents	Speeches for and against smoking
Descriptive:	My grandmother	My dream car: the Porsche 925
Own choice:	About myself	Alien landing

These lists are obvious fictions, constructed to demonstrate extremes of stereotyped response, and most GCSE folders will make more concessions to a balance of interest. The stereotypes, however, serve to emphasise our point. 'Jill's' writing is more confessional and reflective, dealing with people and emotions, using more private forms. 'Jack' likes fact and action; he uses more public forms. Both would grow as writers if they met the challenge of breaking the mould. Folders which share these limitations are submitted for assessment in uncomfortably large numbers.

The NATE Language and Gender Committee is concerned that girls' and boys' selections are unnecessarily restricted. They don't see either boys' or girls' choices as inherently better or worse; rather, they see a 'balanced diet' of subject matter as appropriate for both sexes.

Differences between girls' and boys' writing preferences have also been found in surveys carried out by the Assessment of Performance Unit. In these surveys, girls enjoyed letter writing and stories; they tended to like writing about their families and their personal experiences; boys were interested in factual, episodic writing assignments. These differences are referred to by Janet White in the final article.

Elsewhere, Janet White suggests that girls' liking for, and ability in, school writing tasks shouldn't give rise to complacency: the processes by which girls become 'good writers' in school do not equip them for those more prestigious careers in which the ability to write well might be thought to confer a clear advantage.[7]

Gender stereotyping in reading material

This conversation was between a five-year-old girl and her grandmother as they looked at a storybook:

Child: *'Who do you like best, the prince or the princess?'*

Adult: *'I don't know, I think I like the princess.'*

Child: *'I like the princess.'*

Adult: *'She's very pretty.'*

Child: *'Yes, she's very pretty. The prince isn't.'*

Adult: *'No, boys aren't pretty. Only girls can be pretty.'*

Child: *'Sometimes the girls say the boys are silly.'*

'There was prince Ronald.

'He looked at her and said, "Elizabeth, you are a mess! You smell like ashes, your hair is all tangled and you are wearing a dirty old paper bag. Come back when you are dressed like a real princess."

' "Ronald," said Elizabeth, "Your clothes are really pretty and your hair is very neat. You look like a real prince, but you are a toad."

'They didn't get married after all.' [8]

. . . a fairy tale ending?

There are now several studies of stereotyping and sexist bias in children's stories, reading schemes and textbooks. They show that female characters — women, girls, and even female animals — are seriously underrepresented in children's books. Female characters also tend to have stereotypical attributes and to be shown engaged in a narrow range of activities, often home-based. Furthermore, at least in older examination classes, young people are presented with relatively few texts by female authors. Teachers have been concerned about the rather impoverished images of women conveyed to children, and often reproduced in their own writing. Several sets of guidelines or checklists have been devised to aid in the selection of school books that show alternative images, and particularly more positive images of women. [9]

However, concerns about sexism in published materials need to be set in a wider context. Images are available from other sources too: at school, in the different career patterns and responsibilities of female and male teachers; in the community, in the different activities engaged in by women and men.

The representation of women and men in the mass media is more stereotyped than in 'real life'. Much of the research on media images has focused on the presentation of women and men in magazine and television advertisements and in television programmes generally. Again, women are underrepresented, particularly in serious roles, and when they are included more attention is often paid to their appearance than to the appearance of male characters. In advertisements, dramas and comedy they tend to be shown in supporting roles — someone's wife, girlfriend or parent — and they have stereotyped occupations — housewife, or a job from a limited range of paid employment. Men, by contrast, are overrepresented; they take leading roles and are shown in a much wider range of situations than women. [10] Another aspect of the media image of women is that they are often the butt of jokes; think of the caricatures of 'the wife' or 'the mother-in-law'. This may be because most cartoonists and comedians are men. Such examples of discrimination are fairly easy to identify, but there are other less obvious ones. For instance, stereotyped images may be subtly reinforced by the way in which we use language to refer to or to describe women and men.[11] Concerns about sexism in children's books and in their own writing have to be seen in this context: from birth through to adult life children are exposed to images of women and men, both obvious and subtle, from a variety of sources. These images pass on messages — that certain kinds of behaviour, appearance, employment are appropriate for either men or women, and that women and men are differently valued in our society, with less value generally attached to 'women's activities'.

In the articles that follow, teachers and National Writing Project co-ordinators describe their attempts to monitor girls' and boys' approaches to writing and to challenge stereotypes such as those described above. The articles have been grouped under two broad headings: 'Investigating children's choices and preferences' and 'Exploring gender issues through writing'. In 'Writing, gender and change: some questions to consider' there is a brief discussion of some key questions arising from teachers' attempts to tackle gender issues. In a review article, Janet White, from the National Foundation for Educational Research, reflects on the work of the National Writing Project and asks whether, in changing the conditions under which pupils write, the Project can hope to effect any lasting changes on *the gendered outcomes of contemporary schooling*. Finally, a diagram devised by Project members raises questions that might form the basis of discussion between teachers who wish to pursue this issue further. A list of references and resources is appended.

The National Writing Project and the National Curriculum

The Project's Development Phase took place before the National Curriculum was formulated. At the time of writing, Statutory Orders exist for only a small selection of subjects, although consultative documents are available for more. What is gratifying is the degree to which the Project has been able to influence developments (especially, though by no means exclusively, in English). There is a high degree of concurrence between the Project's practice as represented in these pages and the aspirations of the National Curriculum. It is not possible at this stage to cross-refer examples of classroom practice in this pack to the Programmes of Study and Attainment Targets in English, Mathematics, Science and other subjects, but the reader is referred to the relevant Orders and Non-Statutory Guidance.

Consultative Group

Richard Bates
Frances Clarke
Gill Clarkson
Ann Davis
Barbara Grayson
Georgina Herring
Nia Pierce Davies
Joan Swann
Barbara Tilbrook
Janet White

1   Investigating children's choices and preferences

With the increasing availability of published work on gender and classroom life, many teachers have begun to monitor what goes on in their own classrooms. The results are often surprising, with differences between girls' and boys' experiences exceeding teachers' expectations. Project teachers and co-ordinators have investigated: the use of writing by adults in the home; young children's preferences for different activities (including writing); and what children choose to write about. They discuss the implications of this work for classroom practice.

Writing in the home

A questionnaire for parents

When Manchester schools entered the Writing Project, one of the teachers' priorities was to prepare a questionnaire for parents and other adults who looked after the nursery and reception children at home. The purpose was to find out about their writing experiences, both past and present. All questionnaires were returned anonymously to school; adults were asked only to indicate whether they were male or female. The adults were asked to indicate what kinds of writing they did at home, and how frequently. Females, it appeared, were far more likely to write messages, letters and shopping lists, and males to engage in writing which was work-related. This explained an apparent discrepancy: the adults also reported that they remembered seeing their mothers write more than their fathers, yet they believed that in their own household both wrote equally. The kinds of writing activity engaged in by females are the kinds more likely to be carried out at home. These are interesting points, and they helped teachers to become aware not only of the kinds of writing their children might see at home, but also of how boys and girls might identify the kinds of writing it would seem appropriate for them to do.

Monitoring young children's activities

Teachers studying aspects of children's behaviour have found it useful to observe children over a period of time.

Nursery children's choices

The six nursery teachers involved in the Manchester National Writing Project took a close look at the choices young children were making. We wanted to find out whether the activities available were appealing to and stimulating all our children, or if some children were not taking advantage of the provision. We were, of course, particularly interested in writing.

We decided to use a simple matrix checklist, with the children's names down one side and the activities along the top. One member of staff was to be responsible for approximately fifteen minutes' observation three times each day for a period of three weeks. They were to note where each child was during that period, indicating children who were unsettled with an 'M'. In the two sixty-place nurseries, each member of staff was to follow just five children more intensively for the same period. At the end of three weeks, when all the teachers had completed their surveys, it became obvious that any general conclusions would be impossible; there was much inconsistency from day to day and from nursery to nursery. Moreover, we had not identified criteria for the selection of children. However, the surveys were of great use to the individual teachers. I did a detailed analysis of the figures from two of the smaller nurseries. I chose the smaller ones because they were easier to compare, and these two because they had maintained quite a consistent approach to their observations, and had identified their full-time children as the ones to be monitored. They will be referred to as Nursery 1 and Nursery 2. Although the staff looked at the full range of activities, the ones I looked at in detail were writing activities, construction, painting and home corner. I was obviously interested in the writing activities, and I selected construction activities and the home corner as I found that in Nursery 1 these were the most popular choices. I selected painting as the fourth area because it is a mark-making activity like writing, but I wondered if it might hold a wider appeal for the children.

I used the staff's tallying as a basis for taking a closer look at the children's preferences. In Nursery 1, the activities of nineteen children were recorded, ten girls and nine boys. I recorded the number of times each child was to be found in each of the four specific areas during the three-week period, during the observation times. The staff had managed to observe twice or four times a day for eight days, a total of twenty-six spot checks. The highest number of times any one child was observed in one of the four areas was fifteen. Although there were almost equal proportions of girls and boys, there was a total of twenty female appearances and only eight male appearances in writing activities. In the construction area there were sixty-five male appearances and forty female ones.

Another way in which I used the figures was to gain an approximate idea of the time individual children were spending in specific areas. Although one girl was counted as being in the writing area seven times and another five times, most of the girls seemed to be found there three times and every girl made at least one appearance. Half the boys did not use that area at all during observations, and only two made more than one appearance. In the construction area girls were each counted as being there between three and five times. No boy appeared less than four times and two were counted there fourteen and eleven times respectively, which suggested that these boys were spending about half of their time there. Only two of the boys and only four of the girls were found doing any painting. Half the girls were spending approximately a fifth of their observed times in the home corner — five or six appearances — and all appeared there at least once. Four of the boys did not go there at all, and only two were seen there more than once. The staff were surprised at the imbalances in these figures, and agreed that the following areas needed looking at in order to ensure that all children experience the full range of activities and make more informed choices:

- the quality of provision in writing and painting areas

- adult involvement across the range of activities

- the status accorded to the different activities

In Nursery 2, the staff had already given considerable thought to the quality of provision and the balance of activities. They observed full-time and part-time children, but only the full-time ones, ten boys and seven girls, are recorded here.

These children were observed three times each day for twelve days. There are twenty-nine recorded appearances by girls in writing activities and only twenty-two by boys, although there were three more of them. It is more difficult to compare these figures because of the imbalance in numbers, but the greater number of boys cannot alone account for there being over twice as many appearances by the boys as by the girls in the construction area — thirty-six to seventeen. As individuals, only two boys were not seen in the writing area, two were seen four times and the rest were seen two or three times each. In construction, three boys were observed there more than three times, and all were seen at least twice. Each girl appeared there two or three times. The painting area was used more in this nursery, with all the girls appearing once or twice and boys between once and three times. These figures obviously present a much greater balance than the figures for Nursery 1, and suggest that the staff's awareness was creating a situation where most of the activities appealed to most of the children. They were surprised that imbalances were appearing as much as they did, and decided that a similar kind of monitoring could be introduced on a regular basis while they tried new strategies to create a greater balance in the future.

Georgina Herring, Project Officer, former Manchester Writing Project Co-ordinator

Girls and boys writing in the nursery

Since we became involved in the Writing Project two years ago we have tried to encourage all children to write through practical activities. We have noticed little difference between boys and girls at this stage, when given a variety of purposes for writing which are firmly rooted in the real demands of our society. This was evident during last term when we embarked on our most ambitious project to date: the school's fiftieth anniversary. Our general topic was about 'Change', and we chose the area of home life in the 1930s. We started with the children's own experiences of family life; parents and grandparents were involved so it became a family topic in a real sense.

We began with a visit to the North-West Museum of Science and Technology where we saw artefacts from the period in contemporary settings. The children were interested in the 'old-fashioned' cars, wireless sets, wash tubs and televisions, and the experience evoked memories of childhood in parents and grandparents. The interest and support generated by the parents following this visit reinforced the work in school as it developed. In the nursery we set up a 1930s home, using original artefacts borrowed from various sources. The children experienced the items fully, winding up gramophones and even washing clothes with a washboard and dolly tub!

In the nursery at St. Aidan's RC Primary School, Manchester, it was noticeable that boys and girls seemed equally interested in writing and very eager to write. Sheila Kearney, the teacher, writes about the way she runs her nursery.

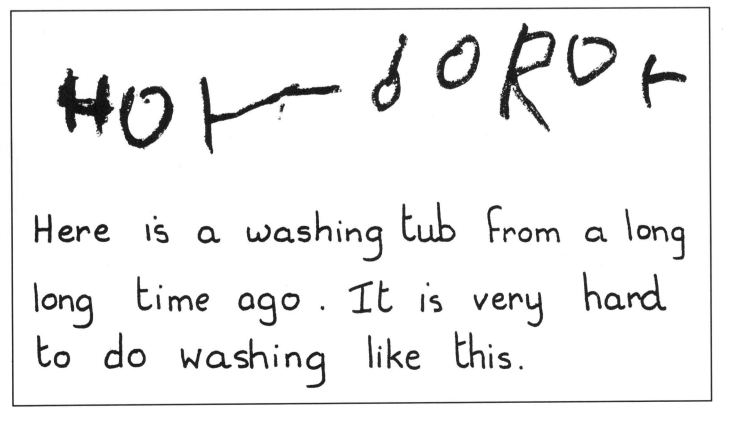

HOT dOROT

Here is a washing tub from a long long time ago. It is very hard to do washing like this.

The children recorded their responses to these experiences on paper, either immediately or later, with reference to photographs. Their recordings varied from marks on paper to full sentences, using enough conventional devices for adults to be able to read the writing. Girls and boys demonstrated equal enthusiasm in their responses to this topic.

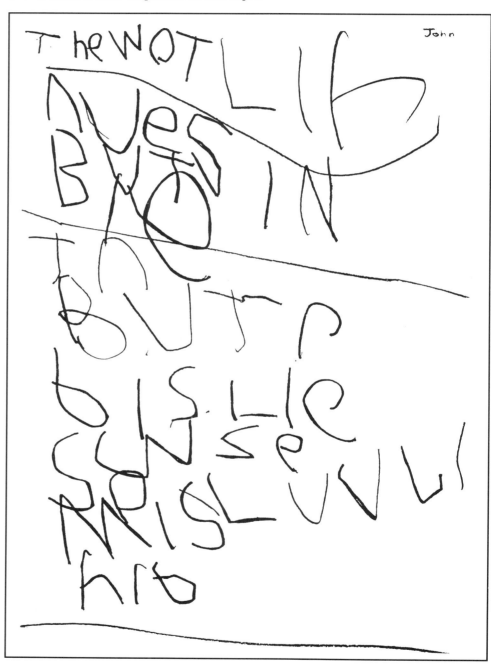

Clearly, the constant parental participation played an important role as they encouraged children to look at and compare objects in the home with those found in the Museum.

Parents also play a central role in our shared writing sessions, coming into the nursery twice weekly. They act as scribes, recording, organising, redrafting and introducing the skills and techniques used in book making. Of course, they also provide writing models. These sessions are given a high profile in the nursery and are open to all children. Although all the parents are female, efforts are made, through an informal rota, to ensure an even distribution of boys and girls experiencing this activity. The finished books are highly valued and given equal status with those of published authors in the book corner. Children are also invited to read them to the class.

Provision is made for non-adult-directed activities; writing areas are equipped with typewriters, assorted writing materials and ready-made books. There is also a low-level message board for children to display letters, lists and messages. In addition, writing materials are distributed in different areas to encourage child-initiated writing. Some children seem to prefer this kind of activity and we try to keep a balance between directed and non-directed activities, always giving support where necessary.

Another topic, again related to the world around us, arose when building work began on the new nursery extension. The children were very excited by this change in our routine and became involved in every aspect of the construction from the planning stage, when the workers noted down measurements and examined plans, to the finished building. We encouraged all the children to make models, draw pictures and write about what was happening around them.

One child, John, who had noticeably grown in confidence as a writer during the 'Change' topic, wrote enthusiastically about the different stages of construction and revealed considerable literary talents previously unknown:

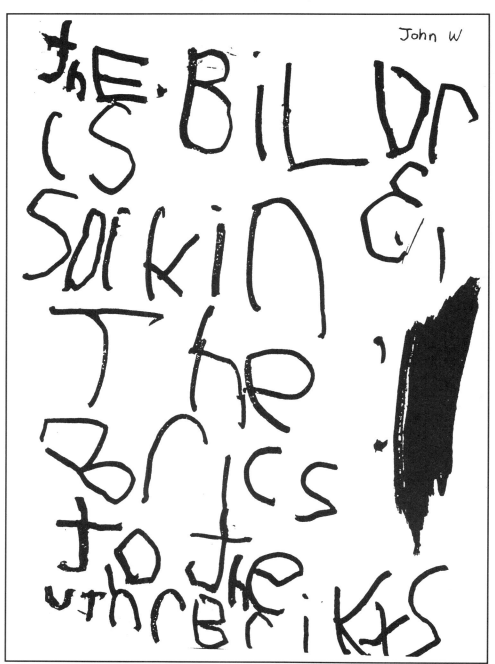

Both boys and girls continue to make their own books, write letters and lists and make captions for models. Their writing is sometimes integrated into a drawing, as they attempt to communicate meaning through print, but often it is a piece of pure writing. Whatever their stage of development I have found it important to provide all children with encouragement and exciting purposes for writing which relate to all aspects of the world around them. I ensure that all needs are catered for and all children actually experience writing. Support from home is also vital in our work, as is the current involvement of adult writing models in our nursery.

Sheila Kearney, St. Aidan's RC Primary School, Manchester

Why is this nursery class so successful in encouraging both boys and girls to write — and to write in unstereotyped ways? Points worthy of attention include the following:

- The children are constantly made aware of adults writing, both the female parents and the male construction workers who come into the school.

- The staff take positive action to ensure that all children experience writing on a regular, informal basis and in an enjoyable way.

- There is constant involvement with parents, which keeps writing a high priority in almost all the children's homes.

- Adults in the nursery generate enthusiasm for writing as a means of communication.

- The children's reasons for writing are based in practical situations, within and beyond the nursery.

Infant children's choices and preferences

There is an area in the centre of the Infant department which groups of children from all Infant classes are timetabled to use. Here, under the supervision of a nursery nurse, they can choose from a variety of activities for which there is no room in the class bases. I decided simply to observe the incidence of children writing in the area: writing in the role-play area, making labels for models, book making and note/letter/message writing. Fifteen out of a possible thirty-five children engaged in writing: two boys and two girls wrote in the role-play area, eight girls wrote letters or messages, one boy wrote a label for a model and two girls wrote computer stories. In the classroom, the kind of writing boys engaged in through choice was writing labels for models and objects from home (both must have labels in order to remain on display for over a day). This showed a very high rate of avoidance on the part of the boys, and I decided to talk to all the children individually.

Using a 'smiley face' drawing I asked each child which two activities this girl (if I was asking a girl) or boy (if it was a boy) would like to choose out of the following: Lego, writing a message, making a book or doing a jigsaw. I used this method because I felt they would be more likely to show their real preferences through the medium of the drawing. Out of eighteen boys, fifteen included Lego in their choice and thirteen included jigsaws, but only six included message writing and two book making. Out of seventeen girls only five chose Lego and nine chose jigsaws, but their figures for writing activities were much higher: twelve included messages in their chosen pair of activities and eight included book making. The world of school seemed to be quite alien to the boys in terms of what they wanted to do (as expressed by a 'smiley face' drawing) and what they were used to doing. When they did choose to write, the writing was for a purpose, with a very definite end in mind, rather than for pleasure in the act of writing. In view of these findings, I have identified several ways in which I could possibly encourage boys to become more involved in writing activities:

- Create more necessity to write by having the children apply to do certain activities through a written request only.

- Introduce zigzag books, using sequenced comic pictures for children to write in the bubbles. (This would introduce the literature boys were used to reading but I would monitor any violence they might try to introduce.)

- Invite more male members of the community into school to become involved in role-play writing and other writing activities.

- Create play areas where both boys and girls may feel they have a place: garage, builder's office, clinic, shops.

St. James' Primary School in Manchester is not one of the Project schools, but it is part of an Authority-wide project involving nursery and Infant classes in many schools. The Early Literacy schools share the same approach to reading and writing as many of the Writing Project schools, believing that children learn to read and write through involvement, enjoyment and experimentation. When Mary Foley, an Infant teacher there, had the chance to 'float' for a term, she decided to observe the two vertically grouped classes of second and third year Infants when they had opportunities for free choice.

The introduction of these things would widen the experiences of all the children.

Mary Foley, St. James' C of E Primary School, Manchester

The articles in the section 'Monitoring young children's activities' mention strategies for encouraging a balanced take-up of activities by girls and boys. You might use these as a basis for discussion with other teachers.

What do girls and boys write?

Through monitoring children's choices of subject matter, teachers have found evidence to support the claim made by NATE's Language and Gender Committee — amongst others — that girls' and boys' choices of writing topics are unnecessarily restricted.

A bit too close to Homer: gender and writing in the Junior school

Last summer, my mixed-ability class of third year Juniors enjoyed listening to a dramatised version of the *Odyssey* which was broadcast in several episodes in a radio programme devised for nine- to eleven-year-olds. After listening to the broadcast each week, the children were free to choose which part of the story they wished to write about. Many of the children proved to be good listeners and often remembered phrases used by the actors, incorporating them successfully in their own retelling of the story.

The class contained thirty-three children: nineteen girls and fourteen boys. Eighty-two pieces of work done by the girls and sixty-six done by the boys were included in this analysis. Some children had produced more than others; this was due to individual differences, absences, and withdrawal of some children from the class on some occasions.

Initially, the children's writing and pictures were mounted on the display boards on two walls of the classroom, with a large figure of Odysseus flexing his biceps and holding his bow on the end wall. All the work done by the children was mounted, not just the best. The children were very proud of their work, and when the day came for it to be taken down there was a general outcry. The cry went up: '*Can't we make it into a big book, Miss?*' I wanted to keep the work, and the children had mounted it on pieces of black sugar paper which were all the same size, so I readily agreed to their suggestion. When I began to compile the sheets to make the book, I noticed that the girls had concentrated on certain parts of the story and the boys on others. (The children had always mixed freely and both sexes were represented on each table.)

The more I looked at this aspect of the writing, the more interested I became. I began to separate the pieces of writing into three broad categories:

- those dealing with emotions (affective)

- those concerning authority, control or personal ascendancy (power-related)

- those concerning physical force or bloodthirstiness (violence-related)

Any piece of writing containing none of these elements was deemed to be neutral. I then carefully analysed each child's work by listing the subjects that the child had chosen to write about or illustrate and then identifying whether they fell into any of the three categories.

It soon became clear that the girls were far more likely than the boys to write about emotions. For instance, after the first episode many girls chose to write about or draw Penelope and her suitors, or Penelope weaving by day and frantically unpicking her work by night in order to delay the moment she feared.

Penelope Weaving
by Shelley Robinett

Penelope is weaving at her tapestry and when she has finished she is going to choose who she is going to marry. Penelope wants to marry Odysseus but he went away. But Penelope has a plan she said that she will weave by day and unpick it all at night. Penelope's father said to penelope the day will come my daughter the day will come for Odysseus to come back.

Angela

Many of the girls described Penelope trying to decide which suitor she was to marry, and mentioned the fact that Penelope was still fond of Odysseus and wished that he would return home.

On the other hand, many of the boys chose to write about Odysseus blinding the Cyclops, Polyphemus, by thrusting a red-hot stake into his single eye, and several drew pictures of Polyphemus hurling rocks at the ships of the departing Greeks. Some boys chose to describe the power struggle and the negotiations between the gods Zeus and Athenae as they decided the fate of the mortals below.

As I looked at the materials, I found more and more examples of girls and boys writing about the same event, but with different emphases. The girls had described the feelings of the people involved, whereas the boys had been more concerned with violence or power. When writing about Odysseus forcing Circe to return his men to human form after she had turned them into swine, one girl concluded, *'Circe asked Odysseus to stay with her but Odysseus told her that he had to get back to his wife.'* Another girl wrote, *'Circe said to Odysseus, "Stay with me and be my love."'* On the other hand, the boys (writing about the same happening) emphasised the power and strength of Odysseus and wrote such things as:

'Then suddenly Odysseus raised his sword.

"Don't kill me," cried Circe. "Who are you really?"

"I am Odysseus, the sacker of cities. Set my men free!"'

Many of the boys' illustrations showed Odysseus as a powerful figure with his sword raised above Circe and one boy had the words, *'Change my men back or I'll cut your head off!'* in a balloon coming from Odysseus' mouth.

After another episode, the girls were obviously fascinated by Penelope's dream and many of them wrote about it. One girl began her piece by writing, *'Ooh-Agh, Penelope woke screaming in bed,'* and went on to describe how Euryclia, Penelope's maid, told Penelope that her dream of Odysseus being in the Underworld was probably true. She wrote, *'Euryclia said that he only lived in her heart.'* Another girl had Euryclia saying to Penelope, *'Go to sleep and dream of a new wedding and a new man.'*

The boys who mentioned Penelope's dream approached it from the point of view of the negotiations between Athenae and Hermes. They seemed to be fascinated by the power possessed by the gods.

'"Hermes, Hermes," said Athenae.

"Yes, what is it, Athenae?" asked Hermes.

"Why did you send Penelope that awful dream?" said Athenae.

"Trickery, sister, trickery and mischief," said Hermes.'

Attitudes to Odysseus' adventures in the Underworld were polarised in the same way. The girls tended to interpret the ghosts as friendly creatures who made remarks such as, *'Hello. Welcome to the Underworld.'* They stressed the comforting nature of Odysseus' leadership and the fact that his men trusted him.

Several of the boys, on the other hand, were fascinated by Odysseus' sacrifice of the goat, the trench of blood and the attempts of the ghosts to drink it. Only one girl mentioned the sacrifice and the blood, and then only briefly in a matter-of-fact way in order to explain the next point she was going to make. The drawings which the boys made of the ghosts in the Underworld almost invariably showed swords attached to some part of their ghostly anatomy, an aspect that was not mentioned in the dramatisation at all.

The girls were touched by the emotional aspect of Odysseus' visit to the Underworld, and particularly by the fact that Odysseus had recognised past family and friends among the ghosts. Here are two examples from their writing:

'Odysseus and his men had been walking when Odysseus saw his mother, and said, "I never thought to see you here!"'

'As he was leaving the Underworld, Odysseus said to his men, "Did you not see any faces you knew and loved?"'

The troubles and temptations that Odysseus met on his journey homewards were also treated differently by boys and girls. The Sirens interested the girls greatly, and their writing contained passages such as:

'"Oh! Oh! come to me, come to me."

"I will, I will, set me free, somebody, set me free."

"Remember me, I was the first one you loved."

"Come to me, Odysseus, come."'

Another girl wrote, *'Odysseus, do you not remember me — I was the love of your youth.'*

Gemma Fay Justin.

The Sirens.

The Sirens, I can hear the Sirens song said Odysseus. The Sirens are in yellow and white. The one in the yellow said "Odysseus, Odysseus do you not remember me," I was the first one that you loved, Odysseus said "I remember, I remember". The other Siren said "Odysseus, Odysseus, do you not remember me I was the love of your youth" Odysseus said "I remember, I remember" Odysseus said "I will come to you". Then Odysseus said "cut the ropes and set me free". But Odysseus men could not hear him!

The boys hardly mentioned the Sirens, concentrating instead on Scylla and Charybdis, and their pictures and writing reflected the violent nature of this part of the story. Many boys repeated the sentence spoken by Odysseus in the dramatisation, *'Charybdis is the danger; she sucks in any living thing and then spits them out again in a bath of blood.'*

Ishanil Martin

Cylla and Caryldis

"I can see rocks captain" said Eurylochus.
"Now keep close to Cylla and row as hard as you can. Cylla will not do anything But Corybdis is the danger, she sucks in any living thing and then spits them out again in a bath of blood so the blind prophet in hell told me to keep to Cylla" said Odysseus.
"Whats that captain I head something" said Eurylochus.
"That must be Cylla" said Odysseus.
Ahhhhh.
"Look at that captain! a 6 headed monster.
Look out, Polites", said Eurylochus
"You tricked us captain. you tricked usss" said Polites
"6 good men, gone. What Polites said was true.

Towards the end of the story, many girls were moved by the death of Argus. They wrote such things as:

'''Argus, you recognise me, all this time you have waited, watching, trusting for me to come back. Argus, Argus, could you not have lived one more day?'''

'"*Oh Argus, my beloved dog. You recognise me after all these years. You must not leave me now," he said.*'

The relationship between Odysseus and Penelope was also of interest to the girls, and some wrote about Penelope's doubts as to whether the returned wayfarer really was her husband Odysseus.

At this point in the story, Odysseus' revenge on the suitors was the most popular subject for the boys. Here is an example:

'"*I am the man thought dead," said Odysseus. "I am Odysseus!!! I'm going to send you all to the kingdom of Hades!"*

Odysseus lunged forward with his mighty sword and began to slay every suitor in sight! One by one they fell, straight to the kingdom of Hades!!!'

The girls wrote about emotions on a total of forty-two occasions, while the boys wrote about them on only five occasions. There was more balance where power relationships (authority, control or personal ascendancy) were concerned. The figures here were twenty for the girls and thirty-four for the boys. Indeed, the girls' portrayal of female characters did indicate their belief that women are strong; this strength was personal, though, and not concerned with violence or political ascendancy. The girls wrote about physical force and bloodthirstiness on four occasions and the boys on eighteen occasions.

However, I do not wish to give the impression that preferences were totally polarised. A minority of girls and of boys were happy to write about the whole spectrum of subject matter.

Conclusions which may be drawn from this analysis

Among this group of children:

- Girls were just over six times as likely as boys to write about affections/emotions.

- Boys were more than twice as likely as girls to write about authority/control/personal ascendancy.

- Boys were just over six times as likely as girls to write about physical force/bloodthirstiness.

Questions

- Does an analysis such as this have any implications for the class teacher?

- Should the class teacher abandon free choice, and seek to influence the children in the type of subject chosen?

- Could the balance be made more even through preliminary discussion?

- Would the same picture emerge if a similar analysis were done at a later stage in the children's development — for example, at age thirteen or sixteen?

Norah Arnold, Ferrars Junior School, Luton

Two sixth formers look at Infants' story writing

Andrea Smallwood and Peter Howe, sixth formers in Dudley, have explored issues of gender through investigating the stories written by one class of Infants.

The class we visited at Tenterfields Primary School consisted of six- and seven-year-olds. The children had been writing stories for the reception class as part of the Writing Project.

We talked to groups of four children for about ten minutes each, concentrating on several points: the story itself, why a particular subject had been chosen, obvious influences (for example, television programmes or books) and the other children's opinions of the finished product.

There were two main categories of story: fairy tales, and gangs or groups. The most remarkable feature was that, without exception, girls chose one type of story and boys chose another. In fact, it would be quite possible to identify the sex of every writer merely on the basis of subject matter. Typical titles of stories by the girls were 'The pretty princess', 'The mermaid', 'The book of Fairyland' and 'The princess party'. Boys wrote stories with titles such as 'The gang', and 'The Dustbin Family'. The substance of most stories by girls tended to be marriage, birthday parties and beautiful princesses, and all the stories had happy endings. Races, fights, spiders, darkness, cricket and cars formed the subject matter of the majority of the boys' work.

The boys' stories were much more aggressive, with one character frequently achieving power over another. The girls placed their heroines in a passive role, subordinate to other characters. The boys created a greater sense of place and spatial awareness, concentrating particularly on the bigness of things. In an excellent story by Alper Dervish about the race to build a spider's web against adverse weather conditions, we are told that Mr. Spider made the biggest web, but his friend made a middle-sized one and got wet.

Is this an indication of a sense of the survival of the fittest, an early idea of the law of the jungle? The only competition that occurred in any of the girls' stories occurred in Ruth Lee's 'Betty the cat'. Here Betty is a ballerina who wins a cup. Before she makes her quite devastating stage entrance, Ruth writes, '*She was scared but she was beautiful.*' Does she believe that a girl is protected by her beauty?

Emphasis was also placed on possessions. Anna Duffield's 'Molly Dolly' lists her Christmas Day gifts as a little pair of dancing shoes, a pretty dress, a necklace, a bracelet and a ring. Princes and palaces were also common subject matter, but it is significant that it was always the prince as opposed to the female character who took the initiative. In Jacqui Evans' excellent story 'The mermaid' the heroine is consoled by a sympathetic queen who allows her to live in the palace.

'So now the mermaid is a princess so she's very happy. She's found a prince to marry.'

The prince said do you want to marry me Pretty Princess I will marry you come in and sit down they kissed each other

from Pretty Princess

All the children enjoyed listening to each other's stories. Both boys and girls appeared to enjoy stories written by both sexes, which is slightly puzzling in view of the very different kinds of subject matter.

As we attempted to discover just why the girls and boys wrote stories on such clearly differentiated subjects, we were surprised to find that they tended to enjoy the same television programmes, and it was only in the books they read that the gender difference was reflected. It was obvious that they identified their own writing with books they had read.

As sixth formers, we were amazed at the high standard of presentation, including that of the illustrations and the cover. Mrs. Fine had previously discussed the idea of writing books with the class, and the idea of 'fruit people' (for example, Philippa Plum) had been mentioned. This proved a popular suggestion for many children. Mrs. Fine had deliberately refrained from influencing the children's choice of subject, and we are sure this freedom was an important factor in the immense enjoyment the children obviously derived from the project. This enjoyment is reflected in the very high standard of the work produced.

One final point is that in adult literature and entertainment, sexism and racism tend to be seen as similar problems. But in the children's stories, although the girls appeared to be quite willing to live in a world that is overtly sexist, there were no racist overtones, and no associations between darkness and evil or lightness and good.

Peter Howe and Andrea Smallwood, Ellowes Hall Sixth Form, Dudley

(The Theme Pack *Audiences for Writing* contains this article and others concerning writing for a particular readership.)

Monitoring children's choices can be quite revealing. It can also promote the search for alternative strategies to encourage girls and boys to explore a wider range of topics. Some of these strategies have been published. For instance, Anne Reyersbach[2] shows how all children may be encouraged to read and write poetry, even if some boys are initially reluctant. The NATE Language and Gender Committee's booklet[6] discusses how a topic such as war, which is often presented from a male viewpoint, can be made more relevant to girls by the inclusion of women's experiences: memories of the land army, nurses' letters from the front, the diaries of women in munitions factories, the memoirs of conscientious objectors and women in the Resistance.

Do interventions by teachers conflict with the principle of allowing pupils to choose what they write about? Or does the teacher, by offering alternatives, broaden the scope for choice? This theme is taken up again in the articles that follow.

2 Exploring gender issues through writing

The study by sixth formers Peter Howe and Andrea Smallwood raised its own authors' awareness of gender issues. The following articles continue this exploration of writing and consciousness raising; they consider, in particular, how one may use writing to question stereotyped notions of masculinity and femininity. With the advent of published studies of gender stereotyping in books, magazines and in the mass media generally, many teachers have found ways of using writing to challenge common stereotypes. Project teachers and co-ordinators have examined traditional gender roles in well known stories and in their pupils' own writing. They have also encouraged pupils to investigate and reflect on gender divisions and inequalities.

Exploring stereotypes

The following three articles describe different ways in which teachers and pupils have discussed and challenged stereotypes.

Challenging stories

With a class of eight- to nine-year-olds, I wanted to explore role stereotyping and children's responses to it. The main focus was on gender roles, although four of our sessions were shared with a small group of physically handicapped children from the adjoining Alf Kaufman School, allowing discussion of stereotyping in relation to handicap. I was interested in the children's ability to recognise stereotyping in the stories they read, their responses to such stereotyping and the ways in which they could use narrative to explore and challenge these issues.

The work began with a reading of *The Turbulent Term of Tyke Tiler*. [12] Three-quarters of the way through I asked the children to draw their impression of Tyke and to guess what Tyke's real name might be. The disclosure at the end of the book — that Tyke is a girl — had a mixed reaction, from disbelief to outrage. Every child had believed Tyke to be a boy. Before discussing this I asked the children to write down their reasons for believing Tyke to be a boy, and any clues they could remember to Tyke's real identity. Their reasons and the discussion that followed were based on statements beginning *'Boys are . . .'*, *'Girls don't . . .'*, *'Boys always . . .'*. The only clue to Tyke's female identity was felt to be the fact that on a number of occasions Tyke was required to help with housework whilst her brother wasn't. The perception that this constituted the female role seemed to be happily accepted by the children.

Following this, the children began talking and writing about their perceptions of gender roles and their responses to them. They explored, for example, the kinds of job they saw as 'male' or 'female', for both children and adults. Where did these role images originate? After lively discussion, most children accepted — some more reluctantly than others — that girls aren't born 'sissies' with dusters in their hand, and that boys aren't necessarily genetically naughtier than girls. The children decided that such images originate in television programmes, books, comics and adults' behaviour at home and at school; the latter was expressed as *'Boys always get done more than girls even when they haven't done anything.'*

The children then looked at, read and discussed a variety of young children's stories, comics, newspapers and magazines. Whilst one group tried to design unisex advertisements, another tried to identify what images of boys and girls were being presented by popular books and comics. Finally, I asked all the

Jan Smith, a teacher in the Rochdale Writing Project, describes her use of a children's book to raise awareness of stereotyping. This led to the children's active involvement in debate, and the decision by some to take action on the portrayal of female and male characters in books.

children to write down what they would say to writers who presented stereotyped images; this resulted in some letters being sent to publishers to complain about role stereotypes.

> In these storys the boy is the main character
> He is brave clever or makes things happen.
> Tom Thumb, Dick, Whitting, Jack and the Beanstalk
> peter and the wolf.

> In these stories girls are the main characters
> but they are not usually brave. They dont make
> things happen themselves and often they do silly
> things and have to be rescued by a man.
>
> Red Riding Hood
> Sleeping Beauty
> Rapunzel
> Snow White
> The Princess and the Pea

The children then decided to rewrite some of the traditional stories they had looked at by changing either the outcome or the sex of the main character. I read them *The Practical Princess*,[13] and they suggested that we should have a copy in school.

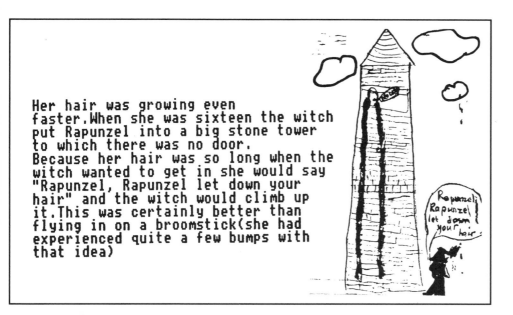

Her hair was growing even faster. When she was sixteen the witch put Rapunzel into a big stone tower to which there was no door.
Because her hair was so long when the witch wanted to get in she would say "Rapunzel, Rapunzel let down your hair" and the witch would climb up it. This was certainly better than flying in on a broomstick(she had experienced quite a few bumps with that idea)

This went on for quite a long time until one night Rapunzel said to her self."I will get out of this place,I don't need a prince with a horse to get me out of here.I've thought of an idea"That night she cut off her hair plaited it and tied it round the hook on the window sill.In the middle of the night down she climbed.She ran and ran.The first house she came to happily was her own.Lilian recognised her and they rejoiced with happiness.

Since the children were also involved in organising a book week and the production of that term's school magazine, elements of the Project work were incorporated into these. They suggested rewriting *The Practical Princess* as a puppet play to perform during the book week, and a particularly heated discussion on gender roles, contributions to which were invariably prefaced with *'I think'*, led to an *'I think'* book and the inclusion of selected *'I thinks'* in the opinion section of the magazine. These related activities required a range of facilities: duplicating machines, computers, craft materials and a variety of audio and musical equipment. Various groups of children were involved in these and associated craft activities such as puppet and scenery making, designing posters, tickets and programmes, and making sound effects and audio recordings.

Shortly after the book week I asked the children to begin a story relating to all the things we had talked about over the past few weeks, but giving no further directions about content, style or message. Noticeably fewer children than before wrote totally single-sex stories, nor did content or likely reader interest seem as closely tied to the sex of the writer as was usual for these children — although many did choose to write adventure stories of the kind which we had looked at and which are commonly found in comics and storybooks popular with this age group. The topic certainly generated lively discussions and a range of writing far greater than was originally envisaged. Over twenty hours were spent on activities directly related to the Project, and on developments from these. The children worked in groups and individually. Some children were involved in nearly all the activities, others in a few. All children in the class participated in at least some of the writing activities and the oral discussions, both class and group, and were in some way involved in the related activities. Much of this project's success lay in the enthusiasm, heightened awareness, excitement and spontaneity that were shared by us all. The work developed in many unplanned ways, often on the initiative of children, and included a much greater range of responses than originally planned. As a stimulus to a wide range of writing activities this project was totally successful, although possibly the most important aspects were the oral discussions, sometimes quite heated, to which children clearly felt that they were contributing as equals; there were no 'right' answers. Through these the children could explore for themselves the issues of fairness and equality, and the influence of written material on attitudes and beliefs.

I think the way the work developed was very much influenced by the children's responses, and I would suggest that the best way to approach work in this area is by not trying to define too closely how you want it to develop. However, I do believe generally that narrative provides a starting point which can stimulate and enable children of this age to engage in issues of this kind. I am quite sure that I could not repeat what happened with this group of children in the same way with another group. Equally, I am convinced that these are issues which are exciting and interesting to explore with Primary children.

Jan Smith, Whittaker Moss CP School, Rochdale

There are many sources of ideas for exploring stereotyping, including gender stereotyping, with children. *Hidden Messages*, produced by the Development Education Centre, gives several suggestions for work on stereotypes in writing and in visual images. Lynn Hayward, in an article called 'Gender and children's writing', describes how she encouraged her Junior school class to explore and challenge traditional fairy tales, as well as engaging in a wide variety of other writing activities.[14]

Scratching the surface

The children's ideas about gender were examined through the medium of writing plays, a very immediate way of bringing a story to life as it relies almost purely on dialogue and action. Furthermore, in encouraging the children to have responsibility for directing their plays and scripting parts, we felt that their thought processes would be made more explicit. The mixed ability group of ten- and eleven-year-olds were aware of their teacher's interest in and commitment to equal opportunities. This point is crucial; it affected not only the teacher's actions in dealing with the pairs of playwrights, but also the children's perceptions of what the teacher wanted them to say and do.

After some general sessions in which the class defined the notion of 'a play' and discussed how to plan and write scripts, they were asked to form friendship pairs, each pair producing a plan for a play which had to involve a family. The participants (pupils and teacher) were to create a fiction in which they would take on roles, negotiating which moments in the fiction to focus upon and how to do so most profitably, and whether they would remain in role, exchange

In this article, Norman Schamroth and Barbara Tilbrook discuss the use of drama techniques to explore gender issues with a class of ten- and eleven-year-olds in a Middle school in Dorset. The article also raises the important question of how far children reveal what they really think in the classroom (rather than what they think is expected of them) and of how far teachers can or should allow their pupils to have a truly free choice.

viewpoints with another character, or reflect upon the proceedings 'as themselves'. Reflection is crucial to the process.

The class formed seven male and six female pairs; none were mixed. The plays of the male pairs included hero-violence stories (4), a fighting-fantasy story (1), an account of a pub fight (1) and a modern day 'disaster' (1). All these plays had males in the major roles and females as submissive or ineffectual minor characters. The plays of the six female pairs included adventure stories (3), a story on the lines of *Animal Farm* featuring domestic pets (1), science fiction (1) and a historically based tragi-romance (1). Four plays featured women in significant and strong roles.

The play we have chosen to look at in detail is the one produced by Alan and Kevin, in which they feature as two young adults involved in drunkenness and fighting.

'I want to make sure that there's rough words in my play and fighting and sport. Me and Kevin are the main characters. We have girlfriends and someone comes along and takes them off us in the pub.'

Two characters who fight to take the girlfriends are called Drunky and Punky, and in the play's original ending the barmaid blamed Alan and Kevin in her statement to the police. The teacher responded in writing to the original plans, and asked the boys each to draw a 'gingerbread' figure to represent the girl characters. They each had to put themselves in the place of the girl characters and write down a brainstorm of their thoughts around the figures. During discussions, it emerged that the boys thought the blame for the fight lay largely with the girls for deliberately trying to attract men (*'The girls were dressed too sexy'*). Alan and Kevin also thought that it was acceptable for the barmaid to lie to the police, and cited personal experience to support both these opinions. It is interesting to note that Kevin was unable to fill in his gingerbread in the first person. He knew he had to write as if he were the girlfriend, Clair, but began his sentences with *'She'*.

Each pair produced a storyboard for their play. The teacher wanted them to concentrate on what the play was essentially about, and what message it would deliver, because that would encourage the children to search for meaning and purpose. When asked to think about the message of their play, Alan and Kevin wrote:

'Stop the girls dressing up sexy because the blokes might want to have sex and the blokes might get attracted to the girls. We prevent girls dressing up too slutty and tarty.'

The scene they chose to script to show this was set in the pub as the two girls walked in.

First version

1 Kevin:	*Look at the state of you!*
2 Melanie:	*What do you mean?*
3 Alan:	*Look at the flippin' state . . .*
4 Clair:	*Well, look at you.*
5 Alan:	*Well at least we don't go nearly topless.*
6 Melanie:	*If you want us to stay then shut up.*
7 Kevin:	*Forget it. I'll buy a drink.*
8 Clair:	*No, I won't forget it.*
9 Alan:	*What the hell do you mean?*
10 Melanie:	*I thought you liked this dress.*

11 Kevin: I do, but not in the 'Dolphin'.

12 Alan: It attracts the blokes.

13 Alan: Oh, let's all just forget it and go home.

14 Melanie: O.K.

15 Kevin: Let's all go back to Alan's house and have a drink there.

16 All of us: Yeah.

The next step was to act out the scene to enable Kevin and Alan to reflect on it. They rejected the offer of two other boys to play their parts in the play and their wishes were respected, although the teachers felt that this would have enabled them to see more clearly the effect of their dialogue. The class teacher had chosen girls with strong personalities to play the girlfriends, Melanie and Clair — girls who spoke their minds, who were adaptable and who had the ability to listen to and respect other people's opinions. Through questions, the class teacher tried to establish what was behind the remarks Alan and Kevin made:

Kevin: 'I like the bit where I go, "Forget it. I'll buy a drink." (Line 7.) Clair goes, "No, I won't forget it." (Line 8.)'

Teacher: 'Why?'

Kevin: 'It goes like someone's in a sweat . . . 'cos . . . (because of Lines 1 and 3) she's in a mood then and when I go (Line 7) she goes (Line 8) in an angry way . . . she got a shock . . . she was in a sweat with us.'

Teacher: 'In her mind?'

Kevin: 'In an angry way.'

Teacher: 'What would she be thinking?'

Kevin: 'Doubt if she'd have a drink.'

Jackie: 'She'd just go home.'

Teacher: 'What would she really be thinking?'

Jackie: 'She's been insulted.'

Kevin: 'Yeah, about how she dressed up.'

All the time, the class teacher was trying to get the boys to reflect on how the girl characters felt and what might have motivated them. By the end of the session there had been some interesting changes and additions to the script, from Line 11 onwards.

Final version

1 Kevin: Look at the state of you!

2 Melanie: What do you mean?

3 Alan: Look at the flippin' state . . .

4 Clair: Well, look at you.

5 Alan: Well at least we don't go nearly topless.

6 Melanie: If you want us to stay then shut up.

7 Kevin: Forget it. I'll buy a drink.

8 Clair: No, I won't forget it.

9 Alan: What the hell do you mean?

10 Melanie: I thought you liked this dress.

11 Kevin: I do, but not in the 'Dolphin' where my friends are.

12 Alan: *It attracts the blokes.*

13 Alan: *Oh, let's all just forget it and go home.*

14 Melanie: *I don't know about forgetting it, I'm going home.*

15 Melanie: *No, come on, Clair.*

                    (They go out.)

16 Boys: *Hey, hang on.*

In this version, the most obvious change is that the girl characters walk off on their own instead of leaving with the boys. When the teacher asked whether the girls or the boys in the play had changed between the first and the last version, Kevin maintained that the girls were *'calming down'*. Alan concluded the opposite, and there was an interesting debate about not having to shout to show that you're angry. Encouraged again to think about the girl characters' feelings, Kevin suddenly said:

'They're thinking, "I'm getting fed up with these two". As they walk in, they're feeling happy, they're dressed up nice as they can. I reckon that Alan didn't think when he said, "Look at the state of you". (Line 1.)'

These were significant statements, the first outward signs of seeing the girls' point of view. In order to provide another layer of reflection for the boys and to offer the rest of the class a model for working on their scripts, the group of four performed each version of the script. The audience's brief was simply to observe and to comment on any message they received from the plays. The statements made about each play were noted down immediately and discussed. Although it was apparent to us that the girls were portrayed more positively in the latter version, for the class (not surprisingly considering their age) the play was more about friendship, respect and 'who likes whom'. Perhaps they were influenced by the remarks of their classmates for, in the final phase of the work, these typical concerns of the age group filtered through. However, the teachers wanted Alan and Kevin to continue to see the situation increasingly from the girl characters' point of view, and to this end they tried improvisation, hot-seating, role reversal and finally, to enable individual reflection, diary writing in reversed roles. For all four participants the main issue was friendship and quarrels: how you break up and make up, the peer group pressure factor and an overriding need for conciliations all round — 'happy endings'.

Any shifts or stagnations in understanding can only be surmised from looking at the diaries. Alan (as Clair) shows clearly that he still sees it as a 'girls' ' problem:

'It was because we were dressed up and now I feel a bit sorry for them (the boys) because we might have got them into trouble with the manager of the pub . . .'

There is an element of confusion, something yet to be resolved:

'. . . but circling in my head I feel a bit mad.'

Kevin, too, has conflicting feelings; he blames himself (as Melanie):

'The cause of it was me dressing up like that and Clair . . .'

. . . but also recognises that although the clothing upset the boys . . .

'. . . It was their fault as much as it was our fault . . . the upset was for me and Clair.'

Clearly their pattern of thinking had undergone a disturbance, and from disturbance comes learning. The disturbance may be no more than a kicking up of the dust and a realisation that the terrain will not be quite as before. Much more important is whether Alan and Kevin (and indeed the two girls) will recognise the ground if they ever come across it again, and whether they will be reminded of it or redirected to it by teachers and pupils in subsequent story writing situations and other contexts for learning. The project was undertaken in the belief that only by strategically and sensitively tackling stereotypes as children (or adults) present them can meaningful and long-term change take place, a change of understanding that can be transferred and applied to other situations.

But what of the notion of free choice? Were Alan's and Kevin's characters and scenario the product of a hidden curriculum, in which the children either challenge teachers on risqué topics, or pander to ideas they know the teacher is concerned about? How far, as teachers, do or should we let children develop their own ideas when they include stereotypes? When the material produced is deemed unsuitable and when it prods our sense of morality, what do we do? How far do we consult our colleagues before undertaking sensitive topics, and do we deal with issues as they arise? The answers are bound up with the question of how much teachers and children are expected to negotiate the content of the curriculum (and not just the language curriculum). This class teacher so nearly challenged the boys outright when they penned their first scenario! It must be said that, even in such a climate, verbal and non-verbal manipulations by a teacher are perhaps inevitable. More important must be the recognition that, as teachers, we are responsible for attending to the issues (however they emerge) that do come to the surface. Working from the boys' first ideas, we could have focused on violence or the morality of being truthful, but because of the nature of this project we chose gender.

Reaching a greater understanding of the children we work with is a vital way of informing what we think the children need to know. As the investigations with Alan and Kevin unfolded, there was an increased knowledge of them as individuals. The role of the teacher was to ensure that the children were given the opportunity to gain alternative perspectives on their work but with, of course, no guarantee that their learning would be the same. Without reflection the possibilities of learning are squandered, yet children often tend to see their work as an end in itself. In order to encourage them to be reflective, stimulating strategies must be found, hence the drama techniques. The boys could never really be the girls, yet at least they 'wore their shoes' briefly, allowing them to write from the girls' point of view and informing, more fully, their experience.

Norman Schamroth, Dorchester Middle School, and Barbara Tilbrook, Joint National Oracy Project Co-ordinator and former National Writing Project Co-ordinator. (With thanks to the head teacher and Barbara Grayson for their support.)

Gender and writing in the Secondary school

A sixth form CPVE group had been examining how advertisements and romantic magazine stories often perpetuate traditional gender roles. The pupils began to look at ways in which some stereotyped roles could be challenged, by writing short stories in which males displayed characteristics often associated with females, and females displayed those often associated with males. The following extracts are from Tracey Knott's humorous account of a disastrous first date:

'It was June the sixteenth. Today was a very special day for him. For her it was just another ordinary day.

'The day started off badly for him. His alarm didn't go off, his toaster virtually exploded, his car wouldn't start and when he went for the bus he missed it. He arrived at work late and had never seen so much work in all his life. On the way home he got on the bus, only to find he didn't have any change, so he walked. He walked briskly home; his new shoes blistered his feet. He was too nervous to eat. He ran the water for a bath. His bath water was cold and he'd run out of shampoo.

'"Why today?" he thought. "Why me?"

'Nothing had gone right for him all day; he was totally on edge. He looked at

At President Kennedy School and Community College in Coventry, pupils working with their teacher Maggie Hawker have explored gender issues through their writing.

the clock; it was quarter to seven. He opened his wardrobe and pulled out his new suit. He couldn't believe his eyes. Why hadn't he noticed it before? He picked up the suit in disbelief and threw it back down on the bed in anger. How could the rip have got there? He didn't know and at the time he didn't care. He was panic-stricken; he turned and looked at his other clothes in his wardrobe. After trying on at least seven different outfits, he decided on a suit he'd had for a couple of years. It was presentable, but it didn't totally satisfy him. He quickly put on his clothes and shoes. He looked in his full-length mirror. His shoes were clean, his trousers were well pressed, his shirt was brilliant white, his jacket fitted perfectly. He was quite content until he looked at his face. He didn't look at all well; he was nervous. He looked rough and he soon realised why. He'd forgotten to shave. He ran into the bathroom, pulled off his jacket and started to shave. Two small, dark red drops fell on to his brilliant white shirt. He frantically looked for another shirt. He put a small bit of toilet roll on to his cut to absorb the blood. He changed his shirt and brushed his thick, dark hair back into place. He checked his appearance again in the mirror. He still looked and felt awful. He so much wanted to impress this woman. He blushed at the thought. He had always been shy, even at school. Now, at the age of twenty-eight, he was as nervous as ever. He felt as awkward as an adolescent.

'The tall grandfather clock downstairs chimed once.

'"It must be half past seven," he thought.

'He reached for his gold watch and confirmed his thoughts. Anxiously he ran to the window, tripped and fell. Where was she? He checked his watch for the date. It was the sixteenth of June and it had just gone half past seven. He slowly climbed down the stairs, sank into his black leather armchair and sighed loudly. After all of this she wasn't going to turn up. Humiliation came through in a great sweat. He wanted to shout out his anger, but there was no use. "I probably wouldn't have got on with her anyway," he thought. "I'm not bothered." A tear stung his eye; he tried to blink it back. There was no point. Minutes later he was crying like a baby. He hardly heard the knock on the door.'

It is sometimes difficult to make the female character into more than a man with a woman's name, and the male character into more than a woman with a man's name when attempting this, but this writer has succeeded; we never lose sight of Gareth as male and Gayna as female in this story.

'The engine ran smoothly. Gayna talked most of the way. She was very vain and incredibly sure of herself. Gareth felt vulnerable in her presence, but he admired her already. The car park was full, so they parked in a nearby street. There was a strange atmosphere as they walked towards Dortons, as there always is on that first date. The entrance was very grand.

'"We have a table booked for nine o'clock; Anderson's the name," Gayna said. "Is it all right if we go into the bar for now? We'll come back at nine."

'"Whisky and water for me and . . ." she turned to Gareth. "What would you like?" Gareth hesitated. "Erm . . . I . . . I'll have just a tonic water please."

'"Are you sure?" Gayna asked. "Wouldn't you like anything stronger?"

'"No, thank you," he replied.

'They sat down. Gayna talked. She seemed to have such an interesting life, thought Gareth.

'"Right then, tell me something about you," she said. She was definitely in charge.

'Gareth tried to gulp down the lump in his throat.

'"Well, I'm . . . I'm . . ."

'"Hold on," Gayna interrupted. "I've just spotted some friends — sorry, but I must go and say hello."

'She went off, leaving Gareth alone. The butterflies in his stomach were getting worse. He didn't like sitting at the bar on his own. Ten minutes later Gayna came back with two other women.

'"I've asked them to join us — I hope you don't mind," she said.

'"No, of course not," Gareth said timidly. He blushed. As he did so, he felt a slight sting on his face. He couldn't remember if he'd taken the bit of toilet roll off his face. A cold sweat flushed through his body. He wiped the sweat off his forehead and gulped. What should he do? Surely someone would have said something if they'd see it. He thought for a second and then said quietly, "I'm . . . I'm just going to the gents."

'"Pardon?" said Gayna.

'Gareth felt as if his face was on fire. He felt nervous, vulnerable and totally lost.

'"I'm just going to the gents," he said, a little bit louder than before.

'"Oh all right, I'll see you in a minute then," said Gayna.

'Gareth limped to the toilets. He was shaking all over. When he entered he went straight over to a mirror. He gave a sigh of relief as he looked at his face. There was no tissue on his face and he was glad. He nervously smiled to himself. He looked at himself again in the mirror. He looked ill. He felt ill. He went pale when he thought of going back into the bar. He tried to pull himself together as he left the gents.

'"Are you all right, love?" asked Gayna. "I didn't think you looked well earlier — are you feeling okay?"

'"Yes, it's just a little hot in here," he said.

'"Right, it's almost time — let's go," Gayna said.

Maggie Hawker, President Kennedy School and Community College, Coventry, with thanks to the head teacher

Some GCSE pupils were asked to submit a discursive essay on 'A woman's place is in the home'. This elicited some perceptive comments from the pupils.

- 'There should be more advertisements which show women as strong and business-minded, just as men are shown (the Volkswagen advert). And get rid of the image that all strong women look like Norah Batty.'

- 'For most women the main reasons for them wanting to go out to work are so that they may have some independence and regain some self-respect and to feel they have achieved something in their own right, instead of being stuck at home with just the baby and kids to look after and the washing machine to watch.'

- 'How often do we see a female barrister? It doesn't matter that this country is run by a woman because the rest of Parliament seems to be dominated by men.'

- 'In the media men are classified as more dominant behind the scenes as well as in front of the cameras. The countless news coverage programmes fronted by men, the rival chat shows in which there seem to be more men as hosts than women . . . even in films and cartoons you always get the men as heroes. Where are the women?'

In the work discussed in the three previous articles, images of women and men in the media, or in children's own writing, formed the impetus for work on gender stereotyping. Gender can be an interesting topic in its own right, producing much discussion as well as different forms of writing. The following two articles provide examples of this.

Investigating gender

Barbara Tilbrook and Denise Wardle from the Dorset Writing Project describe how a survey of toys owned by a class of nine- and ten-year-olds led to some interesting work on gender — and to discoveries about some aspects of writing.

Dear Editor

Our work on children's toys and gender began when one of the boys in my mixed ability class of nine- and ten-year-olds declared loudly that he didn't like looking at girls' toys. This happened during one of our regular 'show and tell' sessions. I had already sensed intolerance among the boys of some of the items the girls were bringing in, so I decided to tackle the issue. Rather than instigating an unprepared discussion, which might simply have allowed prejudices to be aired aggressively, I suggested a survey of the toys children in our class actually owned. The results certainly showed the boys that the girls had wider interests than they had imagined. All the girls but one, for instance, owned at least one model car. Most of the boys owned cuddly toys.

At this point I happened to read a newspaper article making a Christmas appeal for toys for children, and asking for them to be marked suitable for a boy or for a girl. I took the newspaper into school and it provoked a very heated discussion. Most of the class felt strongly that it was wrong to limit the choice of toys according to the sex of the recipient. Why should all the train sets go to boys? Despite their strong feelings, the children assumed that they were powerless to do anything about this, but I suggested that they wrote letters to the editor of the newspaper. All but five of the children did so. I selected letters making as many different points as possible, and sent them with a covering letter.

I wondered about the kind of response we would get, but I certainly did not expect the phone call which came the following day, asking whether a reporter and photographer could come to interview us.

Although sympathetic to our point of view, which was after all to be the main point of the article, the reporter deliberately challenged the children and tried to provoke them, with particular reference to the boys' fondness for cuddly toys. The boys defended themselves strongly and also objected to a suggested pose for a photograph which would have shown them with fists raised at each other. The article eventually appeared across the centre pages of the newspaper. The children were naturally very excited and intrigued to see how their words had been used and how they had been described.

'"All toys are for both boys and girls," wrote an outraged Heather Fry, age 9.'

The children were able to identify subtle differences between what had been said and what had been reported. I, for instance, had pointed out that boys usually spoke more in discussion; this had been interpreted as:

'But she admitted that the boys are usually more assertive in class than the girls.'

The article aroused a great deal of interest within the school community. Some parents stopped me in the street to express their approval. A parallel class in another Dorchester Middle school wrote to us to express support, and this developed into a letter exchange.

I felt that the children had gained a great deal from this experience:

- Their confidence as first years grew enormously.

- Their confidence and their ability to express their views forcefully but calmly in discussion also increased. (Throughout this work on gender, four or five boys remained totally unconvinced and retained their original opinions, but the rest of the class learned to stand up to them and they accepted that they were in a minority.)

- The children learned that their writing could provoke a response and effect change.

- They also realised that they need not be merely passive recipients of ideas from the media but that they could influence them.

Barbara Tilbrook, Dorset Writing Project Co-ordinator, and Denise Wardle, Dorchester Middle School

Women at work

Secondary teachers in Hampshire have been looking at the subject of writing and the world of work. I decided that I would investigate, in a minor way, how women cope at work in the late 1980s.

Peter Upward, a teacher from Hampshire, gives a 'warts and all' account of an investigation of women at work in the 1980s undertaken by a Secondary English class.

I began by putting down in note form the way I thought it might work. It would involve the top set of my fourth year group in research, putting together questionnaires, interviewing in pairs or groups, discussing their findings and writing them up. As nine out of the thirty in this class were boys, I was interested to see how they would feel about the project. Would they participate only because I had asked them to, or were there things that they genuinely hoped to learn?

I wrote down some general questions that I hoped we would address during the project.

- Is it harder to get to the top as a woman? Do you have to be twice as good as a man doing the same job?

- What kinds of sexist comment have to be withstood?

- If you are a working mother with young children, do these comments only fuel feelings of guilt?

- Do others at work, particularly men, tend to patronise you, and, if so, how is this done?

The reader will quickly see the biased nature of my stance at the outset. Fortunately, although some of the pupils took up these points, many were equally interested in learning about the jobs themselves and what they entailed. Other areas which I highlighted for possible consideration were: how women coped in what were traditionally male jobs; any examples of sexist behaviour at interviews.

The next stage was to find women who would be prepared to be interviewed, preferably in school but otherwise at their place of work. I jotted down some possibilities:

- head teachers and deputy heads

- doctors

- solicitors

- priests

- bank managers

- personnel managers

- policewomen

- hotel managers

- shop owners

- youth workers

- staff development tutors

Contacting people at work to arrange interviews proved time-consuming and often frustrating, but on the whole people were very happy to participate once I had explained the project. There is a great deal of goodwill in the workplace; employers want to forge closer links with schools and pupils.

While this work was going on behind the scenes, I was explaining the project to the pupils. I told them briefly what we would be doing, how I intended it to work and how I hoped they would respond. We went to the local library and borrowed books which included vivid descriptions of the kind of work that women did during the latter part of the nineteenth century and the early twentieth century. I wanted to give pupils something to whet their appetite. This library resource was largely ignored; pupils did not seem to want to reflect on the past to any great extent.

First, I asked the pupils to write down and discuss what they hoped to gain from the project; what were their specific aims? On reflection, this was my first mistake. Many pupils were unable to decide exactly what they wanted, and so they made either sweeping statements or vague, nebulous ones that were equally inappropriate. I should have known that this would be the case with young people who had never embarked upon such a task before. (The interviewing alone would cause many of them difficulties.)

'I hoped to discover what it was really like to be a woman at work, in what I would call a half-prejudiced society . . .'

'I'm not really sure what I hope to gain from this project; if I find out something interesting then I'll know . . .'

'Through a series of interviews I hope to establish whether women think they are harassed, underpaid, overworked or generally treated differently.'

'. . . how a woman has to cope . . . by asking for a description of a typical day, hours worked and personal feelings about the job, their views on equality . . .'

'. . . to compare working today with working forty years ago . . .'

'Do women still want to stay at home and do the housework? Are women still expected to participate in feminine jobs?'

'. . . to see if women really are making a go of it . . .'

'. . . to find out why women have to cope with the combined pressures of everyday life at home and at work . . .'

'I'd like to know if women have become more ambitious or not. Or do they still keep back from promotion for the sake of their husband and family?'

'Did women work because they wanted to or were they forced to work?'

'As well as colleagues' attitudes I was also interested to discover the public's views on women in male jobs; I was hoping to discover if in general the public preferred women in senior positions in the community rather than men . . .'

Many responses were well thought out and laudable, but others failed to take into account the limited number and range of possible interviews, or to consider how such aims could be achieved. Few pupils reflected or discussed enough at this important planning stage.

Some, like Cathy, soon saw the potential in the task:

'When I first started this project, my main aim was to discover if women were discriminated against in their job situations, but it soon became apparent that that was not all I could gain from the project, and so I stopped concentrating purely on sexism and began to broaden my horizons, in so doing I learned more about the women's jobs, and what they involved, and I gained in knowledge of sexual discrimination, knowledge of careers AND knowledge of the real world. After a little prompting, I also began to ask for memorable moments, embarrassing, hilarious or otherwise.'

I mentioned earlier the kinds of job that we would be exploring but I felt it right to use the pupils as a resource too. As well as telling them about the women I would be contacting, I encouraged them to set up their own interviews.

The project began in early November and took about three months. This timespan was forced on us by practical constraints but, on reflection, it was too long: many pupils became bored before the end.

So, how did the project work in practice? I arranged interviews with the following working women: a doctor, a solicitor, a deacon, a personnel manager, a WPC, a police inspector, an RAF sergeant, a staff development tutor in youth work, a deputy head of a comprehensive school, two Secondary head teachers, the owner and the general manager of a personnel services agency and a manager with IBM. Pupils arranged interviews with a pharmacist, a bank manager's assistant/operations officer, a staff nurse in a mental hospital and a bus driver. They interviewed, by letter, a local radio presenter and the Rt. Hon. Shirley Williams MP. Quite a few pupils interviewed their parents and grandparents too.

I felt that the range of jobs covered was reasonable; it was the best I could do with my limited resources of time and contacts. I was disappointed that I had not found more women working in industry, and some of the pupils commented upon this too.

As well as putting together their own questions, pupils met the interviewees at the school office and took them to the interview room where they entertained them for the double lesson. (A kind secretary provided a cup of coffee part-way through the session.) In this way I knew that my class was learning something important about the social aspects of the project. My only intervention would be to appear near the end to ensure that all had gone well, to thank our guest and to talk briefly with pupils after she had left. Only once was I summoned by an anxious pupil who said that they had exhausted all their questions and needed help. I obliged by coming into the interview and helping it along while the pupils prepared to carry on. The class must have felt reasonably confident, because hardly anyone asked me even to read through the proposed questions.

As an example of their interests, here is an extract from the list of questions prepared for the WPC.

- *'Could you describe a typical day?*
- *What different ranks are there and which is the highest a woman has reached?*
- *Is the training the same for women as for men?*
- *Are there many working mums in the Hampshire police?*
- *Is policing different around the country and could you arrest someone in a different area if you were off duty?*
- *What do you think of the portrayal of police in programmes such as "The Bill" and "Juliet Bravo"?*
- *What is the attitude of male colleagues towards you?*
- *What is the most rewarding part of the job/the worst part of the job?'*

It would take too long to give a comprehensive account of our findings, but here is a selection of points raised by the interviewees and by the pupils themselves.

Interview with a WPC

'The training is the same as for men but we also have to train at talking to rape victims and dealing with indecency cases.'

'It is slower getting promoted as a woman as we have to compete with men.'

'I'm the first working mum at this local station and there's only one other one in the whole of the Southampton area.'

'Many of my colleagues feel I should be at home looking after the baby.'

'WPCs are not allowed to police football matches.'

'At the local station there are six WPCs and a hundred PCs.'

'We are more talkative, think differently, are better at getting out of tricky situations and are more calm and collected than our male colleagues.'

Pupils' comments on the interview

'She is allowed to restrain a drunken hooligan or an axe-wielding attacker but not to go to a football match!'

'In the case of reporting a death to a member of the public or one of the force it is the women who are expected to go.'

Interview with an RAF Sergeant

'Women seem to be looked upon as silly little girls . . . no matter with whom I work — mechanics, technicians — they treat women very differently.'

'Women have to be more like men to survive. Girls in "dirty jobs" have to be that much better than men.'

'Out of the 95,000 in the RAF only 5% are women.'

'Women cannot go to war because male colleagues would feel they had to "protect" us rather than concentrating on the fighting.'

Pupils' comments on the interview

'A woman with a child is expected to leave unless she can find someone to look after it but would a man in the forces leave work to look after his child? Probably not.'

Interview with a Staff Development Officer/Co-ordinator in Youth Work

'I find subtle prejudice at work.'

'Men seem to assume that promotion is less important to a woman.'

'Men find it easier to talk to women rather than other men about their problems . . . because they think of a woman as less of a threat, because there is no competition.'

Pupils' comments on the interview

'She said generally she found men didn't enjoy work because they feel pressured into work to support the family. Career discussions are often rushed and given little if any thought. Women tend to take more time choosing a career that suits them and that they can enjoy.'

'To gain promotion women need to be ambitious and male colleagues don't expect this . . . a will to succeed is needed to overcome these assumptions.'

Interview with a manager at IBM

'Appearance affects people's attitudes . . . assisting promotion. At first I wore casual clothes . . . it wasn't until I began to wear suits that people started taking notice of me.'

'One of the questions I was asked at interview was, "Why should we employ you when we can get a man to do the job?" '

Pupils' comments on the interview

'She said if you look more like a man you tend to have more chance of promotion.'

'When she first went into the job she wasn't wearing the clothes that spoke for what she does.'

'She only knows of one female with children at management level.'

'She noticed that women in the company all had degrees whereas it didn't seem to matter whether men had them or not.'

At the end of it all, when the interviews had been laboriously written up, the introductions had been fitted in and the whole thing had been mulled over, what conclusions were drawn?

Although some of the findings provided conflicting evidence, it seems that:

- Not all women want to prove themselves at work.

- Very few women reach high status in their profession.

- Although they have the expertise, many women lack the drive and willpower to reach the top of their profession.

- Often, husbands are perturbed by the thought that their wives are earning more than they are.

- Too often, a man is in charge while women do all the hard work.
- In both the Police and the Armed Forces, promotion for women is slower and harder.
- Women are beginning to prove that they are just as good as men.
- Too often, women still find a so-called man's job (for example, HGV driver) impossible to obtain.
- Women don't let other people put them off a career path because of their sex.
- In general, women are prepared to give up their careers for their children.
- Many working women are also wives and mothers, and this adds even more pressure to their lives.

One pupil listed his own conclusions:

- *'Most of the ladies I interviewed had only started work because it was a financial necessity.*
- *They all shared essentially the same values. They were not prepared to be used or trodden on by men.*
- *Women are feeling the need to be financially independent. They are seeking employment to key positions.*
- *In a time when many men are being made redundant, wives need to work.'*

The pupils also assessed what they had learned in a personal sense:

- *'It taught us about women at work, but it also helped us to gain an important ability — to communicate with and interview a complete stranger.'*
- *'I learned the importance of communication, interpretation and organisation.'*
- *'If I could go back and begin the project again, I would ask a lot more questions of a couple of the women.'*

On the whole, I think that the boys quite enjoyed it, although only two reflected at length on the interviews and on their conceptions and preconceptions. One interviewee who owned her own business had suffered at the hands of male employers earlier in her career. Four times she had been overlooked when it came to promotion, and it had not only hardened her but also slightly embittered her. Two boys in the group interviewing her felt this quite strongly. After refusing to say much, one commented:

'. . . the last thing I needed was to have my view analysed and thrown back to me . . . I felt humiliated by her anti-man attitude.'

I believe that most of the pupils benefited from the experience of interviewing people they had never met before. I saw shy pupils visibly gaining in confidence, and several of the interviewees remarked on how mature and sensible the pupils were and how searching they had found the questions.

I would do another project using people at work, and over two-thirds of the class would like to do something similar too — that can't be bad!

Peter Upward, Neville Lovett School, Hampshire

(A shortened form of this article may be found in the Theme Pack *Writing Partnerships (2): school, community and the workplace.*)

3 Writing, gender and change: some questions to consider

The teachers who have contributed to this Theme Pack were reflecting on their own practice: on the writing activities of girls and boys in their classrooms; on their own attempts to take account of gender issues; and on what pupils might have gained from reconsidering traditional attitudes towards girls and boys, and women and men.

The articles have raised many questions, but cannot claim to have provided solutions. It is hoped that they will serve as a starting point for other teachers' consideration of gender and writing.

Several issues run though these articles, and many of them could form a basis for discussion between interested teachers. They include:

Pupil choice versus teacher intervention

Clearly impressed by the quality of the Infant children's work, the sixth form authors of the article on page 26 comment:

'[The teacher] had deliberately refrained from influencing the children's choice of subject, and we are sure this freedom was an important factor in the immense enjoyment the children obviously derived from the project. This, in turn, is reflected in the very high standard of the work produced.'

Although the children enjoyed their work and derived benefit from it, their 'free choice' of topics polarised into 'girls' ' and 'boys' ' subjects along fairly traditional lines. Other articles explore more explicitly this tension between freedom of choice and teacher intervention. What should we do if free choice produces an outcome that we don't find acceptable? The class teacher in 'Scratching the surface' (page 33) makes a more active intervention: he describes his use of drama in education techniques to explore the way in which two male pupils have depicted girl and boy characters in a play. He comments: *'Clearly [the pupils'] pattern of thinking had undergone a disturbance, and from disturbance comes learning.'* The strategy adopted here encourages pupils to think through their own attitudes towards, and perceptions of, girls and boys. Other articles, similarly, suggest that encouraging pupils to reflect on gender, or simply encouraging a greater variety of writing activities, is liberating rather than restricting: it allows one to broaden the range of options open to girls and boys.

Motivation for change

Two assumptions seem to underlie many concerns about gender and writing: that the writing girls and boys engage in, and with which they routinely come into contact:

- limits their choices as writers

- contributes to a general pattern of gendered behaviour and experience, and thus helps to sustain gender inequalities in a more general sense. (The reverse side of this assumption is that writing can be used to help promote social change.)

The second assumption is often left implicit — but it is discussed explicitly by Janet White in her review article (page 49). It's worthwhile for anyone wishing to bring about change to consider carefully their motivations for doing so. Is it unreasonable, or impractical, for teachers to promote social change — or is this a necessary and inevitable part of the job? Can gender differences in writing be acted upon in isolation from other kinds of gender difference and inequality?

Gender and other issues

In 'Challenging stories' (page 29) Jan Smith describes an exploration of images that focused on gender but also considered disability.

How far is gender 'special', and separable from other forms of social inequality? Sometimes a focus on one topic, such as gender, may seem justified. On other occasions, it may be worth exploring the connections between gender and other topics such as disability, race, class, and cultural differences generally. Can one focus on gender without falling into the assumption that the experiences of all women and of all men are the same? On the other hand, how can one handle explorations of gender and race, for example, in a sensitive way? It is all too easy, in discussing the experiences of different groups, to reproduce certain stereotypes.

Awareness raising or unobtrusive change?

In the nursery described by Sheila Kearney in 'Girls and boys writing in the nursery' (page 15) there seems to be a reasonable balance in the activities pursued by girls and boys. The general awareness of staff, and certain specific provisions, such as having a rota for shared writing sessions, probably contribute towards this. Other articles consider what arrangements may be required to produce an environment that encourages both girls and boys to write in a variety of ways. Other teachers have involved children, particularly older children, more actively in discussions of topics such as gender stereotyping. Rather than simply changing what's available to girls and boys, pupils are made aware of gender issues. Jan Smith, in 'Challenging stories', comments: '. . . these are issues which are exciting and interesting to explore with Primary children'. This awareness-raising strategy also seems to be at work in 'Dear Editor' and in 'Scratching the surface'. 'Two sixth formers look at Infants' story writing' provides a further example in that the sixth formers who investigate younger children's stories are learning for themselves about gender imbalances in the classroom. Can gender imbalances in writing (or other activities) be combated effectively simply by encouraging children to make wider choices? When is it appropriate to bring gender out into the open as a topic for discussion and investigation by pupils? Is this more appropriate for older children?

In the next article, Janet White reflects on the work of the National Writing Project. One or two of the issues mentioned above reappear in this article, which may provide a further stimulus for discussion and debate.

4 Questions of choice and change

'Girls may find sciences boring and keep away, and so never know if they could succeed — it's the same with boys and English.'

How far is it possible that the work of the National Writing Project, in changing the conditions under which children learn to write, might also effect changes in practice in language teaching on a larger scale? Is it possible that children who learn to write under different conditions may also write different texts, and in so doing begin to challenge the conventional links between gender, literacy and ultimate career orientation (girls into the humanities, boys into the sciences)? In the course of this article I want to look at some of the ways in which the Project has encouraged the power and authority of authorship to be handed over increasingly to the pupils, and at the same time made more prominent the relationship between writing and the other language modes. My particular concern is that we do not lose sight of the potential which such changes have for questions of gender identity, and that in celebrating pupils' 'freedom of choice', we do not overlook the role of the teacher in managing the framework in which choices are made.

There are anomalies in the ways in which literacy values are communicated to pupils. For example, as teachers working in the Project have confirmed, from the very start of schooling girls tend to choose writing rather than other learning activities, and they select affective forms of writing — personally expressive accounts, narrative and literary criticism — which are especially prestigious in school terms. Boys typically read and write much more non-fiction, and when they do write narrative, they derive themes of fantasy and violence from comic books and television — sources of inspiration which mark an aspect of counter-culture as far as the mainstream of English teaching is concerned.

Within school, many boys underachieve in reading and writing, and in an education system where formal qualifications depend overwhelmingly on written examinations it is not surprising that more sixteen-year-old boys than girls leave without any qualifications. Nevertheless, once in the 'real world', the girls find that their success in fulfilling school criteria for literary excellence does less than might be expected to advance their career prospects. On the contrary, the process of becoming a good writer at school is, in my view, part of the general sorting process of education whereby girls cease to compete in other fields of work and study, joining that part of the workforce which Acker has described as *'low-paid pedagogues in schools or unpaid domestic pedagogues at home'.*[15]

For girls, the problem does not seem to be the process of learning to be literate, but the kind of literacy they learn and its relationship with talk. Cora Kaplan offers a perspective on the ways in which speech and writing come to be juxtaposed in the lives of many girls:

'. . . speaking up, at home, at school, on the stage, always seemed to involve a sense of danger and challenge which I fed on. Writing, on the other hand, was, to begin with, an act of conformity with family and school . . . all the unspoken pressures and desires on and for me as a precociously clever child were towards channelling my talents into some kind of writing. Talking . . . got me into endless trouble.'[16]

'Finding a voice' is likely to present different challenges for girls and boys.

Research has increasingly drawn attention to the fact that in classroom interactions it is the sheer volume of boys' talk that ensures success of a different, more salient kind when questions of personal value are at issue. Given that so many of the newer approaches to writing allow for purposeful discussion of the writing process, and provide time for pupils to negotiate their intended meanings, how easy is it for these occasions of talk to come to serve as the model for more equal conversations between boys and girls in class — even when the subject is not writing?

Are boys more ready to listen and girls more ready to talk in co-operative ways thanks to the experience of serving as readers and critics of each other's work? When response partners or collaborative groups are used for writing, how much mixing of the sexes is there? How are the roles of participants negotiated? This leads us to consider the teacher's role: in the 'process classroom' the role for the teacher is more varied, more exacting, than outward appearances might lead one to suppose . . .

'No longer are they writing to tell the teacher something the teacher already knows, or simply because the teacher tells them to. If the situation is real, their writing has real authority. They have something to say to the world at large and they no longer need someone else to tell them how to say it. They have become more independent, no longer inferior partners in the reader/ writer relationship. They have learned that, in the real world, writing is about power.' (Margaret Wallen in *Audiences for Writing* in this series.)

At the local level of classroom and school, we might well be persuaded that the pupil-centred approach of the National Writing Project — starting from where the pupil is, finding subjects for writing that are close to the needs and questions of the learner, addressing readers who are known and responsive, developing editing practices based on the actual writing of pupils — is a way of giving pupils power, at least in the sense of experiencing the process of decision making that surrounds the act of composition. Power in that sense is notably absent from traditional practices of writing in unison, on prescribed themes, for undefined audiences and minimally defined purposes.

The extent to which we might wish to go along with wider generalisations about authorial power tends to be qualified when we attend to the content of what children are in fact writing in the name of 'free choice'. Pupils draw on a relatively limited experience of written texts: those which form part of the daily life of the classroom, things which they happen to have read, or choices stimulated by the interests of the peer group. The print environment is saturated with stereotypes of all kinds, and in the absence of sensitive teacher management this will limit the choices of young authors even more.

Professional alertness to the problems of gender-biased material is constantly being sharpened in relation to texts for reading. Curiously, though, we seem to have been slower to realise that once children's own texts began to be produced and circulated for class consumption, we had opened the door to an unchecked rehearsal of problems similar to the ones associated with movements to widen the range of reading material.

Alongside the building up of class libraries, there has been an increased use of excerpts and passages chosen for the vividness of their appeal and their usefulness in stimulating wide-ranging discussion or writing. No one would deny the value of much of the vigorous work that has stemmed from this material, but the choice of passage, the emphasis in discussions and the tasks set have been chosen primarily to respond to the apparent interests of the pupils, which may be exaggerated versions of current prejudice.

'Thus it could be that movements in the teaching of English designed to make literature more accessible to a wider range of pupils and more closely

attuned to pupils' own concerns have actually had the unintended effect of allowing the presence of society's sexual role stereotypes an easier passage into the classroom.'[17]

Apart from the telling studies discussed in this volume, mention might be made of other instances where *'society's sexual role stereotypes'* have had *'an easier passage into the classroom'*, because of the limitations of the questions pupils can set for themselves about different genres of writing.

The first of these instances comes from two of the many class projects focusing on writing stories for younger readers. An older child would be introduced to a younger reader, who then outlined the type of story (s)he would like to have written. The 'writer' took notes at one or more interviews, before producing a tailor-made story. In some cases the final products were word processed, but all were attractively produced and illustrated. The pairing of readers and writers was done on a random basis in terms of sex of pupil.

I became alert to the content of the stories when I heard some of the writers (aged nine to ten in one case, and twelve to thirteen in another) talking about the awkwardness of trying to write for members of the opposite sex. I was later struck by the differences between first and final drafts of the stories.

First draft of children's story (collaborative composition)

Squirrel get Lost   23rd March

One day Vanilla the squirrel was liging on her bed crying. because she had no one to play with. and she thought of mobley and chocey. and get up quickly and ran to mobley and chocey's house and knocked on the door but there was no anster so she looked in the window - but there was no one there. so she decided decided to look for them. she was very sad. She looked in the wood but couldn't find them after half an hour she got tost relised She was Lost and Sat by a tree and said I new I would have nobody to play with I mite as well go home. but I don't know the way though. but then she saw some Foot Prints and Folowed them. and soon they came to an end and looked a head and saw chocey and Mobley a sleep. so she went to play with them.

Final draft of children's story

VANILLA GETS MARRIED

On the second of June Vanilla was going to get married to Nutty. She had a fortnight to choose a dress for herself and the dresses for the bridesmaids. Two weeks had passed and she had chosen a lovely velvet dress for herself and silk dresses for the bridesmaids. Everybody in Nutmeg Forest was invited to the wedding in Oakley church.

The great day came. Mrs. Hedgehog was getting the food ready as she loved cooking. They had nutty cream buns, bark pie and lots of other nice things. At the church they had just finished decorating it with lovely flowers.

Meanwhile Vanilla was putting on her veil while Nutty was putting on his tie. When all was ready Nutty got in the log car. It was a piece of wood with wheels. Everybody was there waiting for the bridesmaids and Vanilla. Vanilla's dad was bringing Vanilla down the aisle. The little squirrels looked very sweet in their bridesmaids' dresses and they carried a lovely basket with flowers. In Vanilla's paw she carried a lovely bunch of flowers that her dad had given her. Her dad was in a smart grey suit.

When the wedding reached the end everybody started throwing flower petals all over Vanilla. Then the service finished. "Let's go to Mrs. Hedgehog's house and have the wedding food." "Yes, that's a good idea." They ate all the food then they gave the presents. Vanilla got a lovely lace pinny from Mrs. Hedgehog and some silver knives and forks and spoons from Brock the Badger and other nice things. Her best present was a giant nut from Nutty. When the party was finished Nutty showed her to her new cottage and they lived very happily after after.

First draft of children's story (collaborative composition)

The Man Who wants the money dog
Once there was a dog what was worth alot of money. And there was a gredy man who wanted the Bullseye the dog. One day the gredy man had an idea how to catch Bullseye. The next day the man put a big bone in Bullseyes masive garden when Bullseye was Just going to get his teeth onthe bone the gredy man snachted Bullseye up in a Sack and took him home in is Van and put him in a stonny cage. Bullseye stayed to get out of his cage. The next day the man woke Bullseye up but he was not there So he went into the garden but there was only foot prints so he followed them they lead to the road acoss the road. the wer mens foot leding to a house and behind hind the house there was a field behind but there was Scathing at the door the house was Bullseye with his real onwers. but this was

Final draft of children's story

BULLSEYE AND THE TRAIN ROBBERS

One day Bullseye, the money dog, was going to Crufts Dog Show on a train from Cornwall to London. His owners were tidying Bullseye up. They combed him with gold combs. When they'd finished they put his gold collar on and his silver coat. Suddenly the train jerked forward but luckily nobody was hurt.

The train went for about another 20 miles then it stopped again. Some robbers burst in, wearing balaclavas, and shot a bullet up at the roof of the train. All the ladies screamed and Bullseye barked. One of the robbers pointed the gun at Bullseye. Then he snatched Bullseye by the neck and ripped off Bullseye's gold collar, tore off his silver coat and took his gold comb.

The robber was just about to throw Bullseye out of the window but Bullseye bit him and the robber dropped Bullseye on the floor. Bullseye ran under the seat. The robber was in such pain that he dropped his gun and Bullseye ran out and picked it up in his teeth. He ran towards his owners with the gun in his mouth. Then one of the robbers kicked Bullseye and Bullseye dropped the gun from his mouth onto the floor. The robber picked it up and Bullseye ran back under the seat. He started whining. One of the robbers shouted at the owners to make Bullseye shut up and they made him be quiet. Suddenly a man shouted help out of the window. A robber shot him and opened the door and pushed the man out of the door.

"That is what will happen to anyone who shouts help out of the window!" the robber shouted. Bullseye came out from underneath the seat and tried to get out but the robber just shut the door and Bullseye banged his head on the door. Then Bullseye's owners hear one of the men who were holding them say, "Let's kill them all."

"No, we will hold them for another hour but get rid of that dog."

"How, though?"

"I don't care how, just get rid of him, O.K.?"

"All right, all right, keep your hair on, Bob."

"You wally, Tom, you're not supposed to tell them my name.

Oh! I've just said your name!"

The other robber called them both wallies and said, "Let's get out of here before they call the cops."

"We already have," said a guard.

Then a shotgun went off and somebody went out of the door. Then the train started again.

When they were under a tunnel five gunshots were heard. Two doors were opened. When they came out Bullseye was not there and the robbers had gone. Bullseye's owners fainted. The next thing they knew they were down at the police station being questioned about the train robbery. All they said was "Yes...no...yes...no." They stayed there for about two hours then they went home.

They were worrying if they would ever see Bullseye again. Then they heard a scratching noise. It was coming form the door. So they went and opened the door and there was Bullseye. He was holding one of the robbers by his leg. When they saw the robber they picked him up and rushed him down to the police station. He was pushed into a cell with the other robbers, who had been caught by the police. Bullseye got a reward of £59 and they went home. They were so happy to see Bullseye that they gave him a big bone.

In general, what seemed to be happening was that older girls writing for younger girls were doing their best to exorcise from the first drafts any waywardly androgynous tendencies, and produce instead a tightly gendered heroine, in conformity with classic nurseryland fiction. The outputs from all-boy pairings showed less departure from first drafts (once a picaresque adventure always a picaresque adventure). In the second drafts they elaborated considerably on the action scenarios — again, in conformity with established genres, those of the comic book or the televised serial. In the rare cases where a younger boy had attributed an emotion such as fear or uncertainty to a character, the older boy had revised it out of existence.

In the twelve/thirteen-year-old group, cross-sex pairing produced some authoritative rewritings of another sort, where girls or boys respectively were struggling to accommodate the demands of a genre with which they were ill at ease. Thus, girls who were required to write about piratical adventures or robotic armies or football stars resisted the depiction of violence and destruction, and instead offered moral reflections on the *'capital crime'* of murder, or interpolated homilies about the messiness of sports kits and the need to tell parents what time one expected to be home.

Nick had another long look at the wreckage below him. After a little while he spoke,

"I believe this is the wreckage of Dark Mark's ship," he said, "and it seems that everyone aboard has drowned."

"Oh dear," sighed Pirate Gary.

"Don't say that," shouted Captain Nick, "Dark Mark and his crew were evil men. They killed many people who had never done anything wrong. They stole from the poor aswell as the rich. They deserved what they got, although I hate to say it."

I walked home and as soon as I walked through the gateway, my Mum saw me. She went mad, absolutely mad and I was not surprised. My football kit and tracksuit were filthy, my whole body was caked in mud and I had walked all over her nice clean carpet and dripped mud all over it. Oops!

Mum sent me straight upstairs for a bath while she got the dinner ready. After my bath I crept downstairs and sat in front of the TV. I thought she hadn't heard me come down but she had and she stormed into the living room.

"I want a word with you," she said. "Next time you go training, I don't expect to see a single bit of dirt on your tracksuit, alright?"

"Sorry Mum," I answered meekly.

"That's OK," she replied.

The nature of the power exercised here is that of the matriarch, the keeper of hearth, home and conscience — roles which girls are traditionally socialised to accept.

Boys writing for younger girls who had specified some form of adventure story were resistant to the idea that a girl might simply take over the male role of quester, although she and her friends might temporarily be allowed the status of 'one of the lads':

"You, girls will have 10% each and the rest will be the schools to repair it with because as I thought, it was the schools long lost treasure!" Mr Whacker announced.

A cheer went up for Elizabeth and Helen and they were carried out to the playground on the shoulders of some of the girls. Then the celebrations started. Party poppers that weren't used at Christmas, went off and they were the heroes of the school.

Such stories were free from the constraints of morality or social obligation, but also showed another form of power based on gender roles: quite gratuitously, the boy author would intrude upon the tale by inventing a rival gang (of boys) to tease and plague the girls, or by issuing an ambiguous taunt to the returned heroine:

> In the park or in the streets,
> Not quite knowing who you could meet.
> Going to the local Park.
> The one's that's scarey in the dark.
> The gates reveal a whole new place,
> Just think to yourself 'This is Ace'.

Stories such as these could provide a rich source for further work in the classroom, as illustrated by the study of Infant children's work carried out by sixth form pupils in Dudley (page 26). Unfortunately, many such stories, composed in similar circumstances, are handed on to their readers with only a light trawling for response.

Project teachers have been well versed in the inadequacies of one-shot writing (writing which is written in one session, without planning or revision). We need equally to be aware that even when the whole process of extended composition has been fulfilled, the outcome may be one-shot or incomplete in another sense — it may be writing in need of (critical) reading. It is here that the teacher's role is crucial: only by strategically and sensitively tackling stereotypes as children (or adults) present them can a teacher help meaningful and long-term change to take place. The skills of intervention demanded of the teacher far exceed those demanded of the class, group, or outside helpers; it is one of the often overlooked challenges of allowing pupils freedom to choose.

Giving pupils power over the writing process does not necessarily mean that they are writing more powerful texts, or indeed texts of a type that we would really wish them to own. Blanket ascriptions of power — through ownership of writing — may disguise the fact that all we have helped pupils to own are versions of cultural clichés.

Attending to the development of pupils as writers is only part of what needs to be done if notions of power and authority in language use are to have substance. Literacy is a socially mediated process, in which girls and boys are differently positioned from the start; it remains to be seen whether classroom innovations prompted by the National Writing Project radically change the gendered outcomes of contemporary schooling. At the very least, work which questions the role of writing in the construction of our culture must prompt reflections on much that is taken for granted in the language development of children — in particular, the assumption that it is natural for girls to go on filling relatively passive roles as writers and listeners in school.

Janet White, Researcher, Department of Language and Communication, NFER

5 What are writers made of?

How can teachers help themselves and their pupils to become aware of the expectations and pressures of society? The questions raised on the following diagram may help to focus attention and suggest possible areas for discussion and action.

SCHOOL

Does gender affect:

Resources?

What messages about male and female writers do children get from the materials used in school?
How many books by women writers are available?
What images of male and female characters are conveyed?
What roles of female and male writers are portrayed?

Classroom organisation?

How are groups formed for:

- discussion?
- collaboration?
- response?

Do boys and girls behave differently?
Do they offer and accept different kinds of support and response?

Types of writing?

What topics do children choose to write about?
D   girls and boys choose differently?

Are girls' & boys' curriculum choices affected by:

- the kind of writing that is commonly associated with different curriculum areas? (e.g.personal/narrative as opposed to factual/reporting)
- the kind of writing that is given high status or most valued in school?

The process of writing?

- planning and drafting
- discussing, negotiating, collaborating
- final presentation of writing

Do all children make use of these in the same way?
Is there a difference between boys and girls?

Responses to writing?

Do teachers and children respond differently to boys' and girls' writing?
What does teacher response to writing show about what is valued in writing? Does this differ according to:

- the gender of the writer?
- the gender of the teacher?

COMMUNITY

What messages do children receive about the role and status of men and women as writers:

- from the media?
- from literature?
- from types of writing associated with jobs?

WRITER

HOME

What do children see parents and other adults writing?

Who writes:

- personal letters?
- business letters?
- greetings cards?
- reports for work?
- notes to school?
- shopping lists?
- cheques?

What are parents' views about writing?

What do they expect their children to be able to do as writers at school and at work?

WHAT CAN TEACHERS DO?

They can investigate:

Resources for Writing –

- female and male roles portrayed in resources they use and change the balance if needed.
- the use boys and girls make of resources for writing such as word processors. Is there an imbalance?
- how classroom organisation affects boys and girls as writers. Do groups need to be altered?

Views About Writing

- children's views and expectations of themselves as writers. Do these differ for boys and girls?
- parents' views and expectations of their children as writers. Do they have different expectations for girls and boys?
- their own expectations of boys and girls as writers. Do they assess and respond differently to the writing of girls and boys?

The Process of Writing

- how boys and girls work together as writers. Do girls and boys offer each other different kinds of support and response?
- how boys and girls engage in the process of writing. Do they need different kinds of help from teachers?

What is Written

- topic and content choice. Are boys and girls being given the opportunity to develop emotion and action in their writing? If they are writing in a stereotypical way (Boys – action, violence, lack of emotion; girls – lack of action, passive roles for females) can they be helped to question their attitudes and experience?
- choice of format (e.g. reports, guides, instructions, pamphlets, stories . . .) Do boys and girls experience a variety of these?
- types of writing typically associated with subject areas (factual – Sciences; personal –English). Does this affect the subject choices made? Can types of writing be used more flexibly in different curriculum areas? Would this alter the subject choices of pupils?

WHAT CAN PUPILS DO?

They can investigate:

- role models and stereotypes of men and women (as writers, workers, family members) in books, materials, media.
- perceptions of appropriate writing types and topics for females and males (interviews, questionnaires).
- topics chosen for writing by a class or group (their own or younger children's).

They can act on these investigations:

- write to publishers, authors, manufacturers, advertisers, media.
- re-write traditional stories, developing alternative male and female roles differently.
- change their approach to female and male roles in their own writing.
- engage in drama, role play, writing in the role of the opposite sex.

Barbara Tilbrook and Barbara Grayson — with contributions from Project groups

References and resources

Sources marked with an asterisk contain ideas for work or activities to try out with children.

[1] Kathy Kelly and Sue Pidgeon: 'Girls, boys and reading — an overview' from *Primary Matters: some approaches to equal opportunities in primary schools* (ILEA 1986)*

Primary Matters and its companion volume, *Secondary Issues* (ILEA 1986), are full of ideas for introducing equal opportunities in various areas of the curriculum and in school life generally.

[2] Anne Reyersbach: 'Feelings on show — poetry' from *Language and Gender* in the series *Language Matters* (ILEA Centre for Language in Primary Education 1986)*

[3] This study is reported in 'Maternal behaviour and perceived sex of infant' by Caroline Smith and Barbara Lloyd from *Child Development Vol 49 No 4* (1978)

[4] There have been several studies of various aspects of gender and education and of girls' and boys' achievements.
For general surveys see:

R. Deem: *Women and Schooling* (Routledge and Kegan Paul 1978)
S. Delamont: *Sex Roles and the School* (Methuen 1980)
D. Spender: *Invisible Women: the schooling scandal* (Writers and Readers Publishing Co-operative 1982)
J. Whyld (ed): *Sexism in the Secondary Curriculum* (Harper and Row 1983)
J. Whyte, R. Deem, L. Kant, M. Cruickshank: *Girl-friendly Schooling* (Methuen 1985)
Guidelines for the avoidance of sexism can be found in *Implementing the ILEA's Anti-sexist Policy* (ILEA 1985)*

[5] *An Equal Start: guidelines for those working with the under-fives* (Equal Opportunities Commission)*

This booklet discusses differences between the experiences and achievements of boys and girls, and suggests ideas for introducing the subject of equal opportunities to young children.

[6] NATE Language and Gender Committee: *Gender Issues in English Coursework* (National Association for the Teaching of English 1988)*

This booklet gives suggestions for creating opportunities for a wide variety of writing, as well as looking at other aspects of the English curriculum.

[7] J. White: 'The writing on the wall: beginning or end of a girl's career?' from *Women's Studies International Forum Vol 9 No 5* (1986)

Janet White covers several issues relating to girls' and boys' writing; see in particular her discussion of the Assessment of Performance Unit surveys.

[8] R.N. Munsch: *The Paper Bag Princess* (Hippo Books)

An anti-sexist fairy tale.

[9] R. Stones: *Pour out the Cocoa, Janet: sexism in children's books* (Longman/Schools Council 1983)*

A good survey of sexism and children's books plus a checklist.

[10] For a general review of this area, see:

G. Tuchman, A.K. Daniels, J. Barnet (eds): *Hearth and Home: images of women in the mass media* (Oxford University Press 1978)

[11] For a review of gender and language, see:

J. Coates: *Women, Men and Language* (Longman 1986)

D. Graddol, J. Swann: *Gender Voices* (Basil Blackwell 1989)

The following book provides an annotated bibliography of the area:

B. Thorne, C. Kramarae, N. Henley (eds): *Language, Gender and Society* (Newbury House 1983)

For a discussion of 'sexist language', and a checklist for its avoidance, see:

C. Miller, K. Swift: *The Handbook of Non-sexist Writing for Writers, Editors and Speakers* (The Women's Press 1981)

[12] Gene Kemp: *The Turbulent Term of Tyke Tiler* (Faber & Faber 1977)

[13] Jay Williams: *The Practical Princess and Other Liberating Fairy Tales* (Hippo Books)

[14] The issue of bias (including sexism) in children's books is discussed in the following:

Hidden Messages: activities for exploring bias (Development Education Centre 1986)*

L. Hayward: 'Gender and children's writing' from *Language and Gender* in the series *Language Matters* (ILEA Centre for Language in Primary Education 1986)*

This contains several ideas for practical classroom work on various aspects of language and gender.

[15] S. Acker: 'Sociology, gender and education' from 'Women and education' (eds S. Acker *et al*) in *World Year Book of Education* (Kogan Page 1983)

[16] C. Kaplan: 'Speaking/writing/feminism' from *On Gender and Writing* (ed Michelle Wander) (Pandora Press 1983)

[17] M. Healey, M. Marland (eds): *Sexual Differentiation and the Teaching of English* (report of a working party established by the English Committee of the Schools Council)

See also:

T.P. Gorman, J. White, G. Brooks, M. Maclure, A. Kispal: *A Review of Language Performance 1979-1983* (HMSO)

P. Mortimer, P. Sammons, L. Stoll, D. Lewis, R. Ecob: *The Junior Years* in the series *School Matters* (Open Books)